# THE PRINCE OF PEACE

# The Prince of Peace

FOR
ADVENT AND CHRISTMAS

BY THE
MOST REV. ALBAN GOODIER, S.J.

**ST. PAUL EDITIONS**

*Nihil Obstat.*

    **F. THOMAS BERGH, O.S.B.**
       *Censor Deputatus.*

*Imprimatur.*

    **EDM. CAN. SURMONT,**
       *Vicarius Generalis.*

*Westmonasterii*

ISBN 0-8198-5807-2 cloth
      0-8198-5808-0 paper

Printed in the U.S.A. by the Daughters of St. Paul
50 St. Paul's Ave., Boston, MA 02130

The Daughters of St. Paul are an international congregation of religious women serving the Church with the communications media.

# PREFACE

THIS little book of meditations is but one more of very many. Our minds are all different, our method of prayer is different in every case. On this account it partly is that no prayer-book, still more no single collection of meditations, can hope to satisfy all alike. Nor can it even hope to satisfy any single soul, if that soul expects to find in it what prayer alone can give. All it can hope to do is to suggest such matter as may contain substance, such, too, as may help the soul of prayer in its own way to "raise its mind and heart to God."

Such, then, is the aim of these meditations. The writer trusts that none of the points are mere words; certainly, he thinks, none are merely futile. He has relied upon his own judgment in the matter of selection and expression, feeling that so alone could he hope to give the meditations the vitality that is needed; at the same time he has not scrupled to make use of wiser heads and holier hearts than his own in the choice of his material. Particularly will this be found to be the case by those who are well acquainted with the works of Fr. Coleridge, S.J.

*PREFACE*

It has often been said that some kind of selection from his many volumes is much to be desired; the present meditations at times run parallel with Fr. Coleridge's chapters, at times quote his actual words. Where this has been done, acknowledgment has been made by marks of quotation.

We would ask those who are kind enough to give this little book a place upon their prie-dieu, that they would use it in the spirit in which it has been written. The thoughts contained are necessarily brief, but they are thoughts which may easily be developed. They appeal to the heart rather than to the mind; as such, then, let them be taken. In other words let them not be tested by reading only; let them also be allowed to grow upon the mind and heart. Such an appeal seems necessary; for the writing of another book of meditations, after so many that have been tried and found wanting, must almost appear an impertinence, and must at best be always an anxious thing.

# CONTENTS

## PART I
### ADVENT

| | |
|---|---:|
| The Fullness of Time | 1 |
| The Desired of All Nations | 4 |
| The Prophets | 6 |
| The Prophecies | 9 |
| The Prophecies (continued) | 12 |
| The Types | 14 |
| Foreshadowings of Mary | 16 |
| The Blessed Trinity | 19 |
| The Eternal Word | 22 |
| The Word Made Flesh | 24 |
| The House of David | 27 |
| The Mother of God | 29 |
| The Vision to Zachary | 32 |
| The Spouse of Mary | 34 |
| The Marriage of Our Lady | 37 |
| The Salutation of the Angel | 39 |
| The Trouble of Mary | 41 |
| The Work of the Holy Spirit | 44 |
| The "Fiat" of Mary | 46 |
| Mary Alone | 49 |
| The Visitation | 51 |
| The Magnificat | 53 |
| The Magnificat (continued) | 56 |
| The Magnificat (continued) | 58 |
| The Magnificat (continued) | 61 |
| The Birth of St. John | 63 |
| The Benedictus | 66 |
| The Benedictus (continued) | 68 |
| The Trial of St. Joseph | 71 |
| The Expectation | 73 |

# PART II
# CHRISTMAS

| | |
|---|---|
| The Nativity | 76 |
| The Nativity (continued) | 78 |
| The Angels and the Shepherds | 81 |
| The Angels' Song | 84 |
| The Adoration of the Shepherds | 86 |
| Our Lady's Adoration | 89 |
| The Circumcision | 91 |
| The Holy Name of Jesus | 94 |
| The Holy Name of Jesus (continued) | 97 |
| The Purification | 99 |
| Simeon | 102 |
| The Canticle of Simeon | 104 |
| The Prophecy of Simeon | 107 |
| The Witness of Anna | 109 |
| The Star in the East | 112 |
| The Magi in Jerusalem | 114 |
| The Adoration of the Magi | 117 |
| The Return of the Magi | 120 |
| Persecution | 122 |
| The Flight into Egypt | 125 |
| The Holy Innocents | 127 |
| The Return from Egypt | 130 |
| The Choice of Nazareth | 132 |
| The Hidden Life | 135 |
| The Loss in the Temple | 137 |
| The Finding in the Temple | 140 |
| The Subjection of Jesus | 142 |
| The Growth of Jesus | 145 |
| Our Lady of Nazareth | 147 |
| St. Joseph | 150 |

# THE PRINCE OF PEACE

## PART I

## *ADVENT*

### I.—THE FULNESS OF TIME

*"When the fulness of time was come, God sent His Son, made of a woman, made under the law: That He might redeem them who were under the law; that we might receive the adoption of sons."—Gal. iv. 4, 5.*

*"That He might make known unto tne mystery of His will, according to His good pleasure which He hath purposed in Him, In the dispensation of the fulness of times, to re-establish all things in Christ, that are in Heaven and on earth, in Him."—Eph. i. 9, 10.*

1. GOD had permitted the world to teach itself its lesson. Man had learned what of himself he is, or rather what he is not; what of himself he can do, or rather what he cannot do. Till the "Fulness of Time," till the coming of our Lord, the history of mankind had been the history of blighted hopes, of successive disappointments, of civilizations growing up and ending in collapse. It is true there had been some progress in spite of these collapses. From the

ruins of each succeeding stage man had picked out a few relics to be treasured for the future; and these, gradually accumulated, had formed the material side of the "Fulness of Time." There was also the spiritual side. Out of all these experiences man had learned himself—his own limitations, his own humiliation, his utter dependence on some higher power for any hope of safety. He had learned to aspire to other things than this life of ruins and disappointments could give him. Jews and Gentiles alike had come to yearn for something nobler than had as yet been laid before them; this time of longing was the "Fulness of Time."

2. During all these ages God had been watching; watching and waiting. He knew what was happening in the world; not a sparrow fell to the ground without His knowledge. He had given man free will, to do good or to do evil; He permitted him to shape his life in the world as he would. Some of the consequences of his evil deeds He permitted man to suffer, in himself or in his posterity; and this made the misery of the world. But not all did He permit; had He done so, man would have destroyed himself, corrupted himself off the face of the earth. Instead, the hand of God was ever held out to save him from utter ruin, preventing him here guiding him there, in another place enlightening him, strengthening him, beyond all desert or expectation.

## THE FULNESS OF TIME

3. Man needed to learn the lesson; and even today, like a thoughtless child, man needs to be constantly reminded of it. Like a thoughtless child, with the least success he becomes elated, he forgets his littleness and dependence, he assumes airs, he demands all kinds of rights and privileges, he is impertinent to his master, he will brook no interference. And as with the spoiled child, so with man, the only cure is to let him fall. That teaches him, as nothing else, how very weak he is, how very dependent; it teaches him, too, how dear is the heart of the Master who has permitted it. But with us it is not as with the men of the olden times. They yearned for their Lord through the ages; we have Him in our midst, at hand to help when we plead.

### Summary

1. The training of mankind during the ages before the Incarnation, from knowledge of himself to yearning after the Redeemer.
2. The guardianship of God during all these evil times, drawing man to Himself.
3. The need that man has of having the lesson renewed in our own times; and the help that is ever at hand.

*THE PRINCE OF PEACE*

## II.—THE DESIRED OF ALL NATIONS

*"Thus saith the Lord of hosts: Yet one little while, and I will move the Heaven, and the earth, and the sea, and the dry land. And I will move all nations: and the desired of all nations shall come: and I will fill this house with glory, saith the Lord of hosts. The silver is mine, and the gold is mine, saith the Lord of hosts. Great shall be the glory of this last house more than of the first, saith the Lord of hosts: and in this place I will give peace, saith the Lord of hosts."—Agg. ii. 7-10.*

1. It is not mere fancy of historians which sees in the history of almost if not quite all ancient peoples a certain looking into the future, a certain consciousness of undevelopment among themselves, a certain craving for something which they had not yet got, but which was yet to come to them—a light and more perfect understanding, a power for good, a completion and satisfaction in their own being which would bring them peace and contentment. It is especially marked among the Greeks, that hungry, restless, inquiring, half-despairing people, in spite of their natural gifts and perfections; a restless looking beyond which expresses itself with almost tragic force in their philosophers, and in the terrible agnosticism in which at last St. Paul found them. It is marked no less in the less-romantic Romans, whose very triumphs ring with a sense of dissatisfaction, almost with a determination to make themselves believe they

## THE DESIRED OF ALL NATIONS

had found what they had sought. But the later writers betray the hunger, and Virgil portrays the ideal that ate at their hearts.

2. But if this is true of all the nations, how much more true is it of the Jews. Of all races the Jews are the most hungry-hearted. They were built up upon it in the past; in the pursuit of the ideal they were drawn apart from the rest of the world; and even to this day it may be safely said that this hungry searching, for they know not what, characterizes them wherever they go. They look for the Messiah still; this is the first article of their belief. Now, as in early times, many grow weary of waiting, and seek their satisfaction in other things; but their very weariness does but confirm the truth of that hunger that has been, and that lingers on because it would not eat of the bread when it was offered. "Your fathers did eat manna in the desert and are dead; this is the bread which cometh down from Heaven, that if any man eat of it he may not die."

3. The satisfaction of this hungering, expressed in many ways, is not the least of the beauties of the Old Testament, and finds its echo in the New. There are many parallels to the following, but we must be content with one: "I, wisdom, have poured out rivers. I, like a brook out of a river of a mighty water, I like a channel of a river, and like an aqueduct, came out of paradise, I said: I will water my garden

of plants, and I will water abundantly the fruits of my meadow. And behold my brook became a great river, and my river came near to a sea: for I make doctrine shine forth to all as the morning light, and I will declare it afar off. I will penetrate to all the lower parts of the earth, and will behold all that sleep, and will enlighten all that hope in the Lord. I will yet pour out doctrine as prophecy, and will leave it to them that seek wisdom, and will not cease to instruct their offspring even to the holy age" (Eccles. xxiv. 40-46).

*Summary*

1. The hungering for something discoverable in the ancient civilizations.
2. This specially seen among the Jews.
3. The fulfilment in the coming of Our Lord.

## III.—THE PROPHETS

*"Which of the prophets have not your fathers persecuted? And they have slain them who foretold of the coming of the Just One; of whom you have been now the betrayers and murderers: Who have received the law by the disposition of Angels, and have not kept it."—Acts vii. 52, 53.*

1. There is one fact abundantly clear to and freely recognized by every student of Jewish history, whether a friend of Christ our Lord or an enemy. It is the fact that at His coming

## THE PROPHETS

the air was full of expectation of Him. Something had filled the Jewish people with the conviction that the Redeemer, the Messiah, was to come, that He would come about this time, that such and such would be His circumstances, His characteristics, the marks by which He might be known. It is stamped on the literature of the period; it is stamped still more on the first and last chapters of the life of Him who alone has claimed to have fulfilled the expectation: "That the Scripture might be fulfilled which saith," is a constant refrain. And among the Jews today the same expectation is, as it were, petrified; disappointed at the moment, because they failed to recognize Him after all, they have readjusted their understanding of the expectation, but the expectation still remains, stamped on all their liturgy and creed.

2. This expectation, and the figure of Him that was to be, was very clearly marked. He was to be born of a Virgin. He was to be born at Bethlehem; and yet by an apparent contradiction He was both to come out of Egypt and was to be called a Nazarene. He was to be of the line of David. His birth was to be both a matter of rejoicing and a source of lamentation. He was to grow up a King, and yet He was to be the humblest and the meekest of the humble and meek. He was to be the Saviour, and yet was Himself to perish. He was to perfect the Law, and yet the Law was to be ended by this new

legislation. He was to give meaning to all the symbols and sacrifices, and yet was to put an end to them all. Such clear vision, surrounded by such mystery, made up the dawn of the great day.

3. But if you were to have asked them wherever they had derived this knowledge, they could scarcely have told you. It was part of themselves, part of their nation; it had grown with them and it; the climax of the one was the climax of the other. All the past had told it to them; from the earliest tradition it had been with them as a promise; it had taken personal shape with the patriarchs, with Abraham, and Isaac, and Jacob, and Joseph; in Moses it had been fashioned as a source of national life and of religious practice; it had been symbolized in the Law, in the Temple, in the sacrifices and other rites; the heroes, men and women, succeeding generations, had emphasized one feature or another; the prophets, each in his own day, and according to his own surroundings, had added color or a detail to the picture; and the whole had been preserved in the sacred books as an ever-growing revelation.

## Summary

1. The fact of the expectation of Our Lord among the Jews at the time of His coming is accepted by all students of their history.
2. This expectation was not merely of an event,

or of a person in general, but was detailed in its knowledge of what was to be.

3. This knowledge had gradually grown through the centuries, and had been preserved in the books of the Old Testament.

## IV.—THE PROPHECIES

*"As He spake to our fathers, Abraham and his seed for ever."—Magnificat.*

*"He hath raised up a horn of salvation for us in the house of His servant David, as He spake by the mouth of His holy prophets, who are from the beginning."—Benedictus.*

1. From the beginning was the promise of the Redeemer given; the fall of man was accompanied with the assurance of the "seed of the woman" that should crush the serpent's head. More and more is this promise confined to a particular line. Of Abraham it is said that in his seed should all the nations of the earth be blessed; and the same promise is renewed, in almost the same words, to Isaac, to Jacob, to Joseph, and to Juda, in the last case most explicitly of all: "The sceptre shall not be taken away from Juda, nor a ruler from his thigh, till He come that is to be sent, and He shall be the expectation of nations." Later Moses, as it were, closes this first cycle of patriarchal prophecies when at the end of his life he assures the chosen people that "God would raise up to them a Prophet from among their own brethren like to Himself."

## THE PRINCE OF PEACE

2. With the founding of the House of David a new cycle of prophecies began. The Redeemer that is to be is promised to him and to his line; and to this the Angel appeals in the Annunciation to Our Lady when he says: "He shall rule in the Kingdom of David." Then, when the family is settled, come the great prophecies of detail. First is the prophecy of Isaias, which has always been accepted as foretelling the virgin birth of Jesus. "Hear ye therefore, O house of David," said Isaias to the King, Achaz, who would not listen to his counsel; "is it a small thing for you to be grievous to men, that you are grievous to my God also? Therefore the Lord Himself will give you a sign. Behold a virgin shall conceive and bear a son, and His name shall be called Emmanuel." Whatever be the literal meaning of the text, the prophecy rung as such in the minds of the Jewish people.

3. Then come the other two great cries of encouragement to his countrymen, lifting them up in the midst of their trouble, each as it were bringing to a focus the many rays of light that had shone through the ages past. The first runs: "For a Child is born to us, and a Son is given to us, and the government is upon His shoulder, and His name shall be called Wonderful, Counsellor, God the Mighty, the Father of the world to come, the Prince of Peace; His Empire shall be multiplied, and there shall be no end of peace; He shall sit upon the throne of David and upon

## THE PROPHECIES

His Kingdom to establish it, and strengthen it with judgment and with justice from henceforth and for ever." And the second: "Yet a little while and My indignation shall cease.... And there shall come forth a rod out of the root of Jesse, and a flower shall rise up out of his root, and the Spirit of the Lord shall rest upon Him, the spirit of wisdom and understanding, the spirit of counsel and of fortitude, and the spirit of knowledge and of godliness, and He shall be filled with the spirit of the fear of the Lord. He shall not judge according to the sight of the eyes, nor reprove according to the hearing of the ears. But He shall judge the poor with justice, and shall reprove with equity the meek of the earth. And He shall strike the earth with the rod of His mouth, and with the breath of His lips he shall slay the wicked. And justice shall be the girdle of His reins.... They shall not hurt, nor shall they kill, in all My holy mountain, for the earth is filled with the knowledge of the Lord as the covering waters of the sea."

### Summary

1. The promise from the beginning.
2. The promise to David.
3. The promise in Isaias.

## V.—THE PROPHECIES (continued)

*"Behold I send my Angel and he shall prepare the way before my face. And presently the Lord, Whom you seek, and the Angel of the testament, Whom you desire, shall come to His temple. Behold He cometh, saith the Lord of hosts. And who shall be able to think of the day of His coming? and who shall stand to see Him? for He is like a refining fire, and like the fuller's herb. And He shall sit refining and cleansing the silver, and He shall purify the sons of Levi, and shall refine them as gold, and as silver, and they shall offer sacrifices to the Lord in justice. And the sacrifice of Juda and of Jerusalem shall please the Lord, as in the days of old, and in the ancient years."—Mal. iii. 1-4.*

1. Not only was the Messiah foreshadowed by the prophets in the general way, but details of His life gradually peered through the darkness. Thus one of the earliest prophets told his people that when Juda ceased to be a kingdom, then He would come: "The sceptre shall not be taken from Juda, nor a ruler from His thigh, till He come that is to be sent, and He shall be the expectation of nations" (Gen. xlix. 10). And one of the latest prophets made this time still more definite: "Seventy weeks are shortened upon thy people and upon thy holy city, that transgression may be finished, and sin may have an end, and iniquity may be abolished, and everlasting justice may be brought, and vision and prophecy may be fulfilled, and the Saint of saints may be anointed" (Dan. ix. 24).

2. Another prophet told the place where He

should be born. "And thou, Bethlehem, Ephrata, art a little one in the thousands of Juda, out of thee shall He come forth unto me Who shall be the Ruler in Israel, and His going forth is from the beginning, and from the days of eternity. Therefore will He give them up even unto the time when she that travaileth shall bring forth, and the remnant of His brethren shall be converted to the children of Israel" (Mic. v. 2, 3). We know how deeply this prophecy was stamped into the minds of the Jews, for when the Wise Men came from the East, asking where He was born, at once the scribes and priests gave answer: "In Bethlehem of Juda."

3. Another prophet announced the change that would come over the sacrifices of the law, as if this were to be the final proof that indeed it was He. With the prophecy quoted above, compare this well-known passage from Malachias: "From the rising of the sun even to the going down, My name is great among the Gentiles; and in every place there is sacrifice, and there is offered in My name a clean oblation, for My name is great among the Gentiles, saith the Lord of hosts" (Mal. i. 11). Thus would Christ, when He "was lifted up, draw all things to Himself," uniting in Himself, making fruitful in Himself, all the sacrifices that had been or would be; in this sense "the Lamb slain from the beginning of the world," and to the end, as St. John expresses it.

*THE PRINCE OF PEACE*

*Summary*

1. As the time for His coming drew near, prophets began to say more clearly when that time would be; and the hungering hearts of the faithful Jews were full of expectation.
2. Others began to add in details by which He might be discovered; the place of His birth, the place of His exile, the place of His upbringing, as the Evangelists record.
3. Lastly, at least one other marks the one stamp upon His work: the sacrifice of the new Law.

## VI.—THE TYPES

*"Our fathers were all under the cloud and all passed through the sea, and were all in Moses baptized in the cloud and in the sea, and did all eat the same spiritual food, and did all drink of the same spiritual drink, and they drank of the spiritual rock which followed them, and the rock was Christ. But with most of them God was not well pleased, for they were overthrown in the desert. Now these things were done in a figure to them of us.... All these things happened to them in figure, and they are written for our correction, upon whom the ends of the world are come."—1 Cor. x. 1-11.*

1. It may be safely said that the Jewish people looked upon the words of the prophets as but one source of information concerning the Christ that was to come. Perhaps even it was not the chief source; the more does this seem true if we consider the allusions that are made in the New Testament. To them their whole history was prophetic; their great heroes were prophet-

## THE TYPES

ic; their rites and ceremonies were prophetic; in some way everything eventful seemed to foreshadow Him Who was to be the fruit and perfection of them all. As the saints who came after Him were to be His reflection, so the saints who went before Him were His anticipation.

2. Thus, to take but a few examples, in Abraham was foreshadowed His fidelity, His generosity, His obedience, His unworldliness; in Isaac His prayerfulness and His spirit of contemplation; in Jacob His patient toil, His hope, His unspotted purity and His ruling spirit; in Moses the Father of His people, the Lawgiver of the New Covenant, the Deliverer of the people from bondage; in Joshua the Destroyer of the enemies of God; in Samuel the Prophet of the New Covenant; in David the King of the New Kingdom; in Solomon the Builder of the new Temple; and so on through succeeding generations.

3. So, too, did the chosen people see in themselves and their history signs and figures of Him that was to come. They had been in bondage in Egypt; then this was in some way to be the lot of the Messiah. The Nazarene was a word of consecration; then He would be called a Nazarene. The sacrifices of the Temple were of the essence of their faith, and even of their life as a nation; then of His life, also, the essential feature would be the great sacrifice. This mine is almost inexhaustible; it has certainly never

*THE PRINCE OF PEACE*

been completely worked. For we could now go back upon the almost infinite series of types representing the Christ that was to be in countless ways, from the murder of Abel by his brother, the sacrifice of Isaac by his father Abraham, the selling of Joseph by his brethren, and the saving of the brethren by Joseph in return, the prayerfulness of Moses, the brazen serpent in the desert, the slaying of Goliath by David—in all these the Jews before Christ found matter for contemplation.

*Summary*

1. Besides prophecy strictly so called, the Jews saw in all that went before a figure of that which was to come.
2. Thus in all their heroes, patriarchs, prophets, kings, and great men, they saw traits of the ideal Christ Who would include all.
3. And in their own history, and in many recorded details, they pondered on their significance as shadows of the future.

## VII.—FORESHADOWINGS OF MARY

*"Whence is this to me that the mother of my Lord should come to me?"—Luke i. 43.*

1. Though so little is said of Our Lady in the Gospels, there is abundant evidence both there and elsewhere to show that she too was part of the Expectation of the Jews along with her Son; and reason confirms that the two could

## FORESHADOWINGS OF MARY

scarcely have been separated. When the Angel appeared to her, to announce the Incarnation, he speaks as to one who was accustomed to meditate on ancient prophecies; and six months later she breaks out in words that could only have come from one who recognized in herself the fulfilment of many things foretold. Elizabeth's words, again, disclose one who appreciated to the full the meaning of Mary's motherhood; and Simeon later is even more explicit. Lastly, the tradition of the second Eve was one which the Jews held dear.

2. In the same way, then, as the great men of the Old Testament prefigured the Son, so did the great women prefigure the Mother; and it is to be noticed that the history of the Jews is studded with the names of great women far more than is the history of any other ancient people. Rebecca secured the inheritance for her son Jacob. The mother of Moses saved him from the waters to be the saviour of his people. Anna breaks into her song of praise at the knowledge that she is to be a mother, which song is the background for the greater song of Mary herself. Deborah and Joel each in their turn are the saviours of their people; later come the names of Judith and Esther, each reminding the Jews of that first prophecy: "I will set enmities between thee and the woman, and between thy seed and her seed; it shall crush thy head"; and telling them that in the future the

Mother of Him that was to come would have her share in the work of Redemption.

3. Again, there were the countless other types, of which the Church has made so much use in her prayers and liturgy. The Little Office of her Immaculate Conception is full of them. She is the Gate of Heaven, the ladder of Jacob, by which God came among men. She is the Burning Bush, seen by Moses, the "holy ground" in which God dwelt; as the Church sings on the feast of the Circumcision: "Rubum quem viderat Moyses incombustum, conservatam agnovimus tuam laudabilem virginitatem." ("In the bush which Moses saw burning but never burnt we recognize thy glorious virginity preserved.") She is the Ark of the Covenant, in which the Sacred Bread from heaven was preserved. She is the Tower of David, in which the King took up His abode. She is the Golden Temple, hallowed by the Presence of Jehovah. If we would lengthen out the list, we have but to look at the writings of many of the Fathers, of those especially on whom, as it were, the glorious sunrise of Our Lady's honor shone after the first centuries of the dawning.

*Summary*

1. The Church sanctions, and the Gospels more than justify, the searching for anticipations of Our Lady, as of her Son, in the persons and events of the Old Testament.

2. Thus in the line of great women she is fore-

*THE BLESSED TRINITY*

shadowed; beginning with the thought that she is to be a second Eve, reversing the work done by the first.

3. In many types, too, she is prefigured, making it easy for saints and fathers of the Church to prolong her praises in their prayers and writings; a practice which was common among them.

## VIII.—The BLESSED TRINITY

*"In the beginning was the Word, and the Word was with God, and the Word was God. The same was in the beginning with God. All things were made by Him, and without Him was made nothing that was made. In Him was Life, and the Life was the Light of men, and the Light shineth in darkness, and the darkness did not comprehend it."—John i. 1-9.*

1. The greatest of our mysteries is the mystery of the Blessed Trinity, of three Persons in one God, God the Father, God the Son, God the Holy Spirit. To use the words of the Athanasian Creed: "The Person of the Father is one, of the Son a second, of the Holy Spirit a third. But of the Father, and of the Son, and of the Holy Spirit the Divinity is one and the same, the glory is equal, the majesty is coeternal. As is the Father, so is the Son, so, too, the Holy Spirit. Uncreated the Father, uncreated the Son, the Holy Spirit, too, uncreated. Unlimited the Father, unlimited the Son, unlimited the Holy Spirit. Eternal the Father, eternal the Son, eternal the Holy Spirit.... Omnipotent the

Father, omnipotent the Son, omnipotent the Holy Spirit.... God the Father, God the Son, God the Holy Spirit.... The Father the Lord, the Son the Lord, the Holy Ghost the Lord. Yet not three Lords, but only one."

2. God the Father alone completely knows Himself. He so completely knows Himself that His very understanding of Himself is more than an image. When I know another I have in my mind an image of that other, a perfect reproduction of him so far as my mind can reproduce him, but still never more than an image, however alive with my life it may be. But in God the Father this image of Himself is perfect. He understands Himself so completely that the image of Himself is complete. And as the image in my mind lives by my life, so does the perfect image of Himself in His perfect and all-comprehending mind live by His perfect life—and is; is "the Father's understanding of Himself, begotten by that understanding, in the same identical nature as the Father"; is the Son of God, "born of the Father from all eternity."

3. "The Father beholds the Son, God of God, Light of Light, true God of true God, altogether like to and equal to Himself, and the possessor with Him of His whole Nature and Deity. The Son beholds the Father, the Supreme and Eternal Good, of Whom He is Himself begotten eternally without imperfection, from Whom He receives the Divine Nature and all that He has. Thus

## THE BLESSED TRINITY

the Father loves the Son, and the Son loves the Father with infinite and eternal love. The love of the Father and of the Son is mutual and one, mutual because each Person loves the other, one because the Nature of the two is not twofold, but one and the same. As the intelligence of the Father is infinitely fertile, and generates the Son, so the love by which the Father loves the Son, and by which the Son loves the Father is infinitely fertile, and breathes the Holy Spirit. The Eternal Father and the Eternal Son communicate to the Holy Spirit, by this act of love, Their own whole Substance and Nature, and thus produce, in their Deity, another and distinct Divine Person, the same in Nature with themselves" (H. J. Coleridge).

### Summary

1. The mystery of the three Persons in one God is the sublimest of our mysteries, on which the greatest saints ever loved to meditate.
2. We have an inkling of its meaning in realizing the Son as the fruit of the Father's perfect understanding of Himself.
3. And of the Holy Spirit as the fruit of the perfect love of Father and Son for each other.

## IX.—THE ETERNAL WORD

*"That which was from the beginning, which we have heard, which we have seen with our eyes, which we have looked upon, and our hands have handled, of the word of life: For the life was manifested: and we have seen, and do bear witness, and declare unto you the life eternal, which was with the Father, and hath appeared to us: That which we have seen and have heard, we declare unto you, that you also may have fellowship with us, and our fellowship may be with the Father, and with his Son Jesus Christ."—1 John i. 3.*

1. "All things were made by Him, and without Him was nothing made that was made." Perhaps it would be more accurate to translate: "All things came into being through Him, and without Him nothing came into being that did come to be." If all things come from the mind of the Father, and the Son, the Word, is the complete understanding of that mind, then by the Son, through the Son, all other things come to be absorbed in, emanating from, the more complete concept, as rays of the great sun from their center. The Eternal Word is the center and source of all creation.

2. "In Him was life." Not only in that He is essential life, inasmuch as He is God and Creator, but also in His office of Redeemer, so that "the Life of which he now speaks is the eternal life of grace and glory, which man had lost by his fall, and which is restored to him by

## THE ETERNAL WORD

means of the Incarnation." Thus St. Paul: "According to His own purpose and grace, which was given to us in Christ Jesus before the times of the world, but is now made manifest to us by the illumination of our Saviour Jesus Christ, Who hath destroyed death, and hath brought to light life and immortality by the Gospel" (2 Tim. i. 9, 19). And St. John: "This is the testimony that God hath given to us eternal life, and this life is in His Son" (1 John v. 11); and again and again in His Gospel he repeats the teaching that Christ our Lord is "the way, the truth, and the life" (xiv. 6), Who came "that they may have life and may have it more abundantly" (xi. 25), and Who defined it Himself in these words: "This is eternal life, that they should know Thee the only true God, and Him Whom Thou hast sent, Jesus Christ" (xvii. 3).

3. "The life was the light of men." The Incarnate Son of God came among men, took on human nature, was visible to men, tangible to men, recognizable by men. This was His revelation to men, the light given to men, of that which hitherto had been the life. Hear again St. John: "The life was manifested, and we have seen and do bear witness and declare unto you the life eternal, which was with the Father and hath appeared to us" (1 John i. 2). And our Lord Himself: "The light is come into the world, and men love darkness rather than the light, for their works are evil. For everyone

that doeth evil hateth the light, and cometh not to the light, that his works may not be reproved" (John iii. 19, 20).

### Summary

1. "All things were made by Him, and without Him was made nothing that was made." Jesus Christ the Word, Jesus Christ the completion of the mind of God, Jesus Christ, the source of all creation.
2. "In Him was life." Jesus Christ essential life, because He is God, Jesus Christ the source of all life, natural and supernatural.
3. "And the life was the light of men." Jesus Christ the manifestation of God to man, the light in the darkness, the way, and the truth.

## X.—THE WORD MADE FLESH

*"He was in the world, and the world was made by Him, and the world knew Him not. He came unto His own, and His own received Him not. But as many as received Him, He gave them power to be made the sons of God, to them who believe in His name.—John i. 10-12.*

1. Before He was manifested in His human nature, the Word was in the world. He was in the midst of creation, manifested in it for anyone to see who would. Says St. Paul: "For the invisible things of Him from the creation of the world are clearly seen, being understood by the things which are made, His eternal power also and divinity, so that they are without

excuse," who refuse to recognize Him (Rom. i. 20). And in his discourse to the people of Athens: "God, Who made the world and all things therein ... giveth to all life, and breath, and all things ... and hath made one of all mankind to dwell upon the face of the earth ... that they should seek God, if happily they may seek after Him and find Him: although He be not far from every one of us; for in Him we live, and move, and have our being" (Acts xvii. 24-28).

2. "He came unto His own, and His own received Him not." Not only was the Word manifested to the whole world, and the world as a whole did not recognize Him, but to His own people, the people He had chosen from all others, He was specially manifested; to them He specially came. To them He was revealed in type and prophecy, among them He came and dwelt at the Incarnation, for their good first of all, for the "lost sheep of the house of Israel"; yet from them He received mainly coldness; they did not want Him, therefore they would not recognize Him, therefore they did not know Him, therefore they would have none of Him. So it has been ever since. Men complain that He is not manifest; but it is the will that is wanting, not the intellect. We could see Him if we would; if we would we could become of His own.

3. "As many as received Him, to them He

gave power to be made the sons of God, to them that believe in His Name." On which St. John comments: "Whosoever believeth that Jesus is the Christ, he is the son of God.... This is the victory that overcometh the world, our faith. Who is he that overcometh the world but he that believeth that Jesus is the Son of God?" (1 John v. 1-5). And this sonship is true. "We have received the spirit of adoption of sons, whereby we cry, Abba, Father" (Rom. viii. 23). It begins in faith; it is effected in baptism; it is continued and brought to perfection in the life of grace and the indwelling of the Holy Ghost; it is consummated in the glory of the body as well as of the soul in heaven. "Brethren, you are now the sons of God, but you know not what you shall be."

*Summary*

1. He was in the world—as its Creator, as its Preserver, stamped upon it so that anyone might read His presence in it—and the world knew Him not—because it would not.

2. He came unto His own—in a special manner to His chosen people, through the prophets, and finally *as one of themselves—and His own received Him* not—because they would not.

3. But as many as received Him—no matter who they were—to them He gave power to be made the sons of God—even in this world; in the next world what will it mean?

## THE HOUSE OF DAVID

### XI.—THE HOUSE OF DAVID

*"He shall be great, and shall be called the Son of the Most High, and the Lord God shall give unto Him the throne of David his father: and he shall reign in the house of Jacob for ever. And of his kingdom there shall be no end."—Luke i. 32, 33.*

1. It is wonderful to notice in the prophecies of the Old Testament how, from the time of David onward, they settle down more and more upon the House of David. This at least was to be one sure sign; and so much had it become an essential part of the Messiah, that those who in His lifetime wished to proclaim their acceptance of His miracles and teaching called Him at once the "Son of David." The Angel alluded to it at the first announcement; Zachary proclaimed it at the Benedictus; "Jesus, Son of David, have mercy on me," cried the beggar on the roadside; the enthusiastic crowd on Palm Sunday shouted: "Hosanna to the Son of David"; even Our Lord Himself, when facing His enemies, used this belief of theirs for their confusion. "And the Pharisees being gathered together, Jesus asked them, saying: What think you of Christ? Whose Son is He? They say to Him: David's. He saith to them: How then doth David in spirit call Him Lord, saying: The Lord said to My Lord, sit on My right hand, until I make Thy enemies Thy footstool? If David then call Him Lord, how is He his

Son? And no man was able to answer Him a word: neither durst any man from that day forth ask Him any further questions" (Matt. xxii. 41-46).

2. The genealogy of Our Lord from David, in that imperfect-perfect manner recognized by the Jews, has been preserved to us. When we look at the line we are struck with many things. David himself was a great saint, but also a great sinner, and Our Lord came from that union which had followed on David's great sin. Moreover, "she that had been the wife of Urias" was not even a Jew. So we can follow down the line of His ancestors and notice that there were others of their kind; that though Our Lord provided for Himself a spotless Mother, He by no means provided spotless forefathers. In this, as in many other ways, "He became like to man"; though in Him sin was not, yet so near did He suffer Himself to be allied to it.

3. Again, though the House of David was not suffered to perish, still it was suffered to be buried for centuries in obscurity; for centuries, too, it was a house divided against itself, and only in its undercurrents did the stream flow on. Kings were born of it, and slew each other, and their families were blotted out; while unknown members carried on the line in hidden places, little suspecting in their obscurity that their lives and the families they reared around them were the most precious, the most significant in

all the world. This is to look at life along the plane of God. From the next world how differently will perspectives appear! "The base things of the world, and the things that are contemptible, hath God chosen, and things that are not, that He may bring to nought things that are: that no flesh should glory in His sight" (1 Cor. i. 28, 29).

## Summary

1. The importance to the Jews of Our Lord's time of this prophecy concerning the House of David.
2. The nature of this house is striking. Though God watched over it, He permitted it to be marked with many a stain.
3. Though He watched over it, He permitted it to be buried and to be unknown; and this is one of its glories.

## XII.—THE MOTHER OF GOD

*"The Lord possessed me in the beginning of His ways, before He made anything from the beginning. I was set up from eternity, and of old before the earth was made. The depths were not as yet, and I was already conceived, neither had the fountains of water as yet sprung out, the mountains with their huge bulk had not been established, before the hills I was brought forth. He had not yet made the earth, nor the rivers, nor the poles of the world."—Prov. viii. 22-26.*

1. "The decree of the Incarnation involved the decree that Our Lord should have a Mother. God might have become man in other ways. He

chose to become man in this. He chose Mary from all eternity to be that most beloved and cherished and honored Mother. Mary was to be the spouse of God, a Mother fitted by grace and dignity for the relation she was to bear to Him. Thus the predestination of Mary comes close on that of Jesus Christ Himself, and cannot be separated therefrom. St. Thomas tells us that God could work greater things than any He has actually worked, except in three instances, the Incarnation of the Word, the Maternity of God, conferred on Mary, and the beatitude of man, consisting in the vision of Himself."

2. On this dignity of Mother of God the belief of the Church concerning Mary's sanctity is founded. When God has chosen souls for a special purpose He has given them special graces in accordance with that purpose. Hence as Our Lady's dignity so far transcends all others, whether on earth or in Heaven, the greatness of her graces, and of her sanctity, is but a natural conclusion. "Many daughters have gathered riches; thou hast surpassed them all" (Prov. xxxi. 29). Thou hast surpassed them all, both in the dowry of graces thou hast received to fit thee for thy office, and in thy faithfulness in using thy graces so as to multiply them. In our human experience we sometimes come across a soul characterized not only by the exceptional favor of God, but also by an instinctive corres-

pondence on its part with that favor. It is a beautiful thing; perfect nature made supernatural. Such a soul tells us something of the soul of Our Lady.

3. We know nothing quite for certain of the childhood of the Mother of God. Stories have come down to us, traditions and apocrypha, which may or may not be true; the first certain fact in her life is the Annunciation. But if we do not know the historical events, we know of much that affords matter by which we may understand her. There is the fact of the Immaculate Conception, by which from the first there was no purifying need for Our Lady; the fact of the consequent unceasing growth in grace, so that the Angels themselves must have always bowed down before her; the fact that her correspondence will have implied a beautiful care to protect the treasure God had given to her, so that, as was said of her Son afterwards, "the child advanced in wisdom, and age, and grace before God and men." What a child must Our Lady have been!

## Summary

1. The fact that Our Lady was to be Mother of God implies a corresponding overflow of grace to prepare for so great a dignity.
2. This overflow of grace implies a correspondence on her part; and this means the highest and most beautiful sanctity.
3. We fill up the story of her childhood by the picture of the child herself.

## XIII.—THE VISION TO ZACHARY

*"Fear not, Zachary, for thy prayer is heard, and thy wife Elizabeth shall bear thee a son, and thou shalt call his name John. And thou shalt have joy and gladness, and many shall rejoice in his birth, for he shall be great before the Lord.... And he shall convert many of the children of Israel to the Lord their God. And he shall go before Him in the spirit and power of Elias, that he may turn the hearts of the fathers to the children, and the incredulous to the wisdom of the just, to prepare for the Lord a perfect people."—Luke i. 13-17.*

[Cf. the whole story, Luke i. 5-25.]

1. The story is the first distinct shadow of the great event that is to come. It is cast first upon the Temple, upon the most sacred spot of the Temple, at the most sacred time, while "all the multitude was praying without at the hour of incense," on the most sacred person, the priest Zachary, whose lot it then was "to offer incense, going into the Temple of the Lord," and after the most sacred manner, for "there appeared to him an Angel of the Lord, standing on the right side of the altar of incense." Zachary saw the Angel, "was troubled, and fear fell upon him"; Mary later saw the Angel and "was troubled"; he before the Angel spoke, she after; which helps us to see the difference in their fear.

2. Then comes the foreshadowing of the person, the last of that procession that has "gone before the Lord," stretching from Adam until this time. Zachary's son shall be called John, that is, "the grace of God." He shall be a joy

## THE VISION TO ZACHARY

to his parents, a joy to many; already the note of joy in the Incarnation is being sounded, so resonant later in all the Angels' songs. Then come the characteristic graces with which the precursor is to be endowed. He shall be great before the Lord. He shall be filled with the Holy Ghost. He shall convert many. He shall go before the Lord in the spirit and power of Elias, that he may turn the hearts of the fathers to the children, and the incredulous to the wisdom of the just, to prepare for the Lord a perfect people. This is he of whom Our Lord afterwards said that he was "a prophet and more than a prophet."

3. Zachary feared, and his fear was the fear of doubt. There were apparently insuperable difficulties to the fulfilment of this promise. He forgot that "nothing is impossible with God." Unlike the humility of Mary, which only looked to serve in whatever capacity, his humility hesitated to let God use it as He would. But God had patience; He gave him the evidence he wanted; the evidence of an Angel's witness, and that Angel Gabriel; the evidence in his own dumbness, that he might learn the better how to speak; the evidence in his own secret heart, purifying his humility, and filling himself with consolation as he dwelt upon the words: "Thou shalt call his name John, and thou shalt have joy and gladness, and many shall rejoice at his birth."

## Summary

1. St. John is the last of the line of forerunners of Our Lord. His coming is surrounded with much of the mystery and awe which belongs to like scenes in the Old Testament.

8. The character and description of John are such as to put him apart from other men. Of no one has Scripture said so much; even Our Lord Himself has given him praise that is unique.

3. Zachary, his father, was a saint, yet a saint who hesitated; and God dealt with him severely yet tenderly, inflicting a trial that He might fill him with the greater joy.

## XIV.—THE SPOUSE OF MARY

*"Wilt thou know, O vain man, that faith without works is dead? Was not Abraham our father justified by works, offering up Isaac his son upon the altar? Seest thou that faith did co-operate with his works: and by works faith was made perfect? And the scripture was fulfilled, saying: Abraham believed God, and it was reputed to him to justice, and he was called the friend of God.... For even as the body without the spirit is dead, so also faith without works is dead."*—St. Jas. ii. 20-25.

1. The time being now imminent, it was essential that Mary should be given a husband and a protector. Of this, too, the Jews must have been aware; for it was a traditional desire among the maidens of the chosen people that they might perhaps, when married, be selected to be the mother of the Messiah. If, then, one easily discovers types of Our Lady in the Old Testament, we do not wonder that anticipations

## THE SPOUSE OF MARY

are found of her spouse, St. Joseph. Thus the faithful servant of Abraham, who brought Rebecca from Mesopotamia and protected her on her way; the faithful guardian Mardochai, who protected Esther, and directed her in her great task of saving her people; these and others would seem to foreshadow the Protector of Mary.

2. But most of all is he seen in his namesake, Joseph, the son of Jacob and Rachel; and this anticipation would seem to be sanctioned by the Church in the free use made in her office of the story of one for the glory of the other. Joseph the dreamer; Joseph sent into obscurity in Egypt; Joseph unknown and unnoticed, though coming of a noble line; Joseph the spotless virgin, whose purity could not be sullied; Joseph entrusted with the care of a kingdom, so that "Go to Joseph" becomes the cry of hope for a whole people—one asks oneself of which Joseph these things are said, the old or the new, so perfectly does the type correspond with the antitype.

3. In all these foreshadowings there is much that prepares us for the character and elevation of St. Joseph. Of his antecedents Scripture tells us nothing; even the Apocrypha have less to say of him than of the other two; but this is in keeping with the spirit and nature of the man as he reveals himself in his later action. St. Joseph is the man unknown, the man whose

selflessness is perfect, the man who has no history of his own, but only lives in others, for others, fulfilling the bidding of God. He is prepared from within, perhaps all unconsciously even to himself, for the great dignity that is designed for him—the husband of Mary, the foster-father and guardian of the Holy Child, the patron of the Universal Church. What that preparation may signify or include we may endeavor to fathom in meditation, but we know we shall never wholly comprehend. Still, these things we can assume; the spouse of Mary will himself be the most innocent of men; the Guardian of Jesus will be perfect in wisdom and prudence; the Patron of the Church will be one filled with zeal for the glory of the House of God.

## Summary

1. An anticipation of St. Joseph would seem to be reasonably seen in the Old Testament, as in the servant of Abraham, Mardochai, etc.
2. Above all is it seen in the other Joseph, of whom so much can be said that is equally said of St. Joseph himself.
3. And for his early life, we have abundant matter for meditation in the silent training of the future trusted servant of God.

# THE MARRIAGE OF OUR LADY

## XV.—THE MARRIAGE OF OUR LADY

*"As the Church is subject to Christ, so also let wives be subject to their husbands in all things. Husbands, love your wives, as Christ also loved the Church, and delivered Himself up for it; that He might sanctify it, cleansing it by the laver of water in the word of life; that He might present it to Himself a glorious Church, not having spot or wrinkle or any such thing, but that it should be holy and without blemish. So also ought men to love their wives as their own bodies.... This is a great sacrament; but I speak in Christ and in the Church."*
—*Eph. v. 24-32.*

1. It is not a little thing to realize that Our Lady was really a married woman; that it was as a married woman, the wife of Joseph, and the Angel of the House of Nazareth, that she had for her very own the affection of her Child Jesus; that by this fact she and her Son have proclaimed to all the world the absolute sanctity of the married state, the possibility of rising to the highest perfection in that state, the certainty that for the majority at least the married state is the fulfilment of the Will of God, and therefore the holiest, the purest, the sublimest state of life that they can embrace.

2. On the other hand, in a marvellous way Our Lady has also made herself the model of the state of virginity. Though she was espoused to Joseph, and as such is the patroness of all married women, yet she was bound by a vow to virginity, as is seen beyond a doubt from the

words of her answer to the Angel: "How shall this be, seeing that I know not man?" From this we learn several things; first, that Joseph, too, was bound by the same vow, for Mary could not have so bound herself without the consent of Joseph; in other words, without his own accepting the same obligations. Second, that Mary had, by this voluntary act of renunciation, passed the hitherto accepted boundaries of a woman's aspirations. To be a mother was a great ideal; but, as St. Paul afterwards expounded the doctrine, to be a virgin for Christ's sake was greater. Yet both were holy.

3. Thirdly, the relationship between Our Lady and St. Joseph assumes a certain special degree of love binding the two. There is, then, a sense in which it can be said that Our Lady had a special affection for her spouse, on whatever that affection may be founded. Moreover, it was a human thing, the love that exists between one human being and another. On the other hand it was a selfless thing: "I know not man," implies the foot set firm in refusing any aspect of love that implies mere self-gratification. The perfection of love is the renunciation of its indulgences; this is why true virginity is born of love, and is fed on love, and most easily bestows its love, and unconsciously wins love to itself.

*Summary*

1. Our Lady, as the espoused wife of St. Joseph,

is the patroness of all married life, the model of all motherhood.

2. Our Lady, as the consecrated virgin, is no less the inaugurator and patroness of all religious life, the model in its great renunciation.

3. Our Lady, as one who loved St. Joseph with a special love, and yet remained mistress of herself, is the patroness of all human love, the model according to which its perfection may be attained.

## XVI.—THE SALUTATION OF THE ANGEL

*"And in the sixth month the Angel Gabriel was sent from God into a city of Galilee, called Nazareth, to a virgin espoused to a man whose name was Joseph, of the house of David, and the virgin's name was Mary. And the Angel, being come in, said to her, Hail, full of grace, the Lord is with thee, blessed art thou among women."*—Luke i. 26-38.

1. The evangelist is determined to leave no doubt as to the time, or place, or the persons, or the circumstances concerned. It is the most momentous event in history that he is about to relate in the next few words; therefore he will be emphatic and clear in his statements. The Angel Gabriel is sent, the same who had been sent to the prophet Daniel, because he was "a man of desires"; the same who had been sent to Zachary, to announce the birth of the Precursor, the special Angel of the Incarnation. He was sent by God, who "ruled from end to end mightily, and disposed all things sweetly," and had chosen this time, this place, this soul, this circumstance, for the fulfilment of His master-

work. He was sent to this maiden, to this espoused maiden; and of all things the evangelist will have us bear in mind her name: "And the virgin's name was Mary."

2. "Hail, full of grace, the Lord is with thee, blessed art thou among women." Mary is worthy of an Angel's homage: "Hail"—as the French translate the word, "I salute you." Should not this word alone make her place secure in the hearts of all men? She is "full of grace," the translation we have given to the word which means "finished or perfected in favor"; as if to say: "I salute you, perfect Lady, perfect before men, perfect in the eyes of God. I salute you because the Lord, my Lord, has chosen you out of millions, abides with you in a special sense, is soon in a still more special sense to abide with you. I salute you, because of all the blessed women that the world has seen, you are the most blessed, and the source of most blessing, so that from this moment all generations shall take up my word and call you blessed."

3. With this greeting ringing in our ears it is almost useless to enumerate the countless blessings of Our Lady. She is filled with God as is no other, filled with Jesus Incarnate as is no other, filled with the fruits of a perfect correspondence with grace from her first moment of existence, filled with His twelve fruits, filled with the perfect growth of faith, hope, and charity, filled with cardinal virtues and all

## THE TROUBLE OF MARY

that hinges on them, filled with special graces and privileges of her own, complete immunity from sin, and from anything that could separate her from God, perfect conformity of her every act with the Will of God, Virgin Mother of Jesus Christ, Virgin Mother of all mankind, partaker with her Son in the great work of redemption, exaltation above all creatures and the glory of the human race. It would be easy to multiply this litany.

### Summary

1. The circumstances of the Annunciation are very definite and very clear.
2. The salutation of the Angel teems with meaning in every word; to interpret it aright we need to keep before ourselves the whole teaching of theology.
3. The graces of which Our Lady is full are beyond counting.

### XVII.—THE TROUBLE OF MARY

*"Who having heard was troubled at his saying, and thought with herself what manner of salutation this should be. And the Angel said to her, Fear not, Mary, for thou hast found grace with God. Behold thou shalt conceive in thy womb, and shalt bring forth a Son, and thou shalt call His name Jesus. He shall be great, and shall be called the Son of the Most High, and the Lord God shall give unto Him the throne of David his father, and He shall reign in the house of Jacob for ever, and of His kingdom there shall be no end."—Luke i. 29-33.*

1. It is not a little thing to discover that one

so perfect as Our Lady could be troubled; therefore trouble of some kind is consistent with perfection such as hers. She was troubled "at his saying"; his saying, thus far, had been no more than the wonderful salutation; she was troubled because an Angel had used such wonderful words to her as: "Hail, full of grace, the Lord is with thee, blessed art thou among women"; and in her trouble she asked herself what these words would mean, and why they should be addressed to her. Soon she was to understand; soon she was to glorify God at the thought that this salutation would ring through the world for all time; and it is a joy to me to know that when she hears it from my lips it is a cause of joy to her.

2. The Angel calms her trouble with words that might well have caused fear and anxiety in one less steeped in faith, and hope, and love. She is not to fear, because she has found favor with God; He hath regarded the lowliness of His handmaiden. She is not to fear, because, virgin as she is, vowed to virginity as she is, she is to be a mother; how could this but be a further trouble? She is not to fear, because the Son she is to bring forth is to be the Messiah! what a weight of suffering this must mean! She is not to fear, because she is henceforth to be something quite different from that which she has hitherto been; her life is to be tossed and torn, and no longer left in its utter

## THE TROUBLE OF MARY

and happy solitude. How many a saint has quaked with fear at such a prospect!

3. Then she is given the first description of the Child which is to be hers. She has already long known Him in the prophets, the fruit of her lasting meditations. She has known Him in the depth of her heart, for God has been always very near to her. And now the Angel links on the new knowledge to the old, recalling the prophecies, focussing them upon this Child. First, He must be called Jesus, the Savior. Then, He must be called the Son of the Most High. The first declares His manhood, the second His divinity. Then in Him the prophecies shall be fulfilled: the greatness of which the later prophets have spoken of in so many ways; beyond them the promised possession of the throne of David; back beyond that the fulfilment of the promise made to the house of Jacob; back beyond that again the complete restoration of the Kingdom which has suffered eclipse since the days of Adam. "Of His Kingdom there shall be no end"; we hear the words echoing later throughout the Apocalypse of St. John, the song that thunders in the infinite spaces, roll after roll through all eternity.

### Summary

1. Our Lady was troubled. She was troubled at being so saluted by the Angel.
2. Her trouble is calmed by the assurance of favor

with God, but also of elevation to a dignity which will be no light burden.

3. She is told something of the nature of the Son, man, and God.

## XVIII.—THE WORK OF THE HOLY SPIRIT

*"And Mary said to the Angel, How shall this be done, because I know not man? And the Angel answering said to her, The Holy Spirit shall come upon thee, and the power of the Most High shall overshadow thee. And therefore also the Holy which shall be born of thee shall be called the Son of God. And behold thy cousin Elizabeth, she also hath conceived a son in her old age, and this is the sixth month with her that is called barren, because no word shall be impossible with God."—Luke i. 34-37.*

1. Mary does not ask in doubt, as did Zachary; she asks for the sake of her own guidance. There is in her vow a distinct difficulty in the way of her becoming a mother, and she has need of enlightenment. The answer is complete and clear; yet it does not remove the perfection of Our Lady's act of faith. The Holy Spirit, always with her, would now come to her in a new way, elevating her to a new plane of sanctity. He would supply in her and make perfect whatever might be needed for the conception of the Son of God. Thus from Mary alone would the substance of the Child be formed.

2. Then would come the work of the Father. The body so formed by the power of the Holy Spirit should be taken by the Father to become

## THE WORK OF THE HOLY SPIRIT

the body of His own Son. This is the meaning of the words, "the power of the Most High shall overshadow Thee." Thus does each Person of the Blessed Trinity co-operate. "The Father works the work of power in the union of the Person of His Son to the Human Nature, the Holy Spirit works the work of goodness, beneficence, mercy, and sanctification in the preparation of that Human Nature, and the Divine Son Himself becomes Incarnate, and takes to Himself for ever and for ever the Human nature, the body and the soul conceived in the womb of Mary." Therefore, in the strictest sense, as the Angel emphatically concludes, the Holy One that shall be born of the Virgin Mary shall be called and shall be strictly "the Son of God."

3. The prophecy is confirmed by a new announcement; the greater wonder that is to be is confirmed by a lesser wonder that has actually happened. The connection between the two conceptions comes to us very naturally; the announcement to Our Lady seems to be also a guide to her as to what she is next to do, especially when we see to what it prompted her. And the Angel concludes with a quotation from Scripture, referring Our Lady back to the first of those miraculous conceptions which were a type or anticipation of this, that of the barren Sara in the tent of Abraham, when at the promise of the Angel she became the mother of Isaac. And as St. Paul says of Abraham on this occa-

sion, so, and even more may we say of Our Lady: "In the promise of God he staggered not by distrust, but was strengthened by faith, giving glory to God, most fully knowing that whatsoever He has promised this He is able also to perform."

*Summary*

1. Mary asks for guidance, not because she doubts, but because, as is so often the case, to the human mind there is an apparent contradiction in the designs of God.
2. She receives for answer the explanation of the operation of the Blessed Trinity in the work of the Incarnation.
3. And the promise is confirmed, first by the announcement of another miraculous conception, then by reminding her of those conceptions of which this is the antitype.

## XIX.—THE "FIAT" OF MARY

*"And Mary said, Behold the handmaid of the Lord be it done to me according to thy word. And the Angel departed from her."—Luke i. 38.*

1. The Angel had spoken three times. First he had showed the deepest reverence for Mary; and to this she had answered nothing, but disturbed in mind, had pondered much and waited. Then he had announced to her the great message with which he had been entrusted; and to this Mary had replied by quietly asking "How?" Lastly, he had explained the work of the Blessed Trinity in her. In a special way

## THE "FIAT" OF MARY

she understood; she, who, as seen from many infallible signs, was steeped in the Scriptures; she who by the special grace of God, and by her own incomparable innocence of soul, was endowed with special clearness of vision; she who, by exercise in the school of prayer, possessed in the fullest degree that "spiritual understanding" so much prized by St. Paul. Mary was the first to hear and to grasp the great revelation of the New Gospel; the mystery of the Blessed Trinity, and the Incarnation.

2. Her answer is prompt and decisive. There is no hesitation, such as even a saint might have made. Each word is full of meaning. Her readiness and joy in making herself the instrument of the designs of God are shown by the first word, "Behold!" Her profound humility reveals itself in the term by which she speaks of herself: "The handmaid of the Lord." This word also conveys her reason for consenting. Great as was the honor, wonderful the grace, glorious the station on earth and in heaven to which she was invited, she accepted them for no other reason than because such was the will of God her Lord and Master. The words "Be it done unto me" show her marvellous faith. For the Angel had not said she was to do this or that; but that she was to be in a manner passive, though willingly so, in the execution of the great mystery. And the last expression, "according to Thy Word," shows her faith and

humility, as also her joy that the accomplishment of the work was to be brought about in the manner which increased instead of diminishing or impairing the glory of her chastity.

3. This "Fiat" of Mary is more than her own word. It is the conclusion and fulfilment of all her own longings, and of all the longings of all the holy souls that had preceded her since the days of Eve. "Let it be done, Let it be done," had been the prayer of all the ages, and at last the word had been said which was the "Amen" of the litany. She speaks in the name of all the world, in the name of all creation; for her "Fiat" is the acceptance for them of that union with God for which, as St. Paul says, all creation yearns. She stands between heaven and earth, linking the two together, the channel through which God chooses to pass from His throne to the cottages of men, the Mother of divine grace, the Cause of our joy, and all because she had the simplicity, and therefore the unconscious courage, to accept the call of Him who loved her: "Behold the handmaid of the Lord, be it done to me according to Thy Word."

*Summary*

1. Mary understood in a special way the significance of the mysteries declared to her by the Angel.
2. Each word in her answer reveals secrets of her heart and soul.
3. Her "Fiat" is the fulfilment of the longings of all time, of all creation; the acceptance of her station as Queen of all saints.

## XX.—MARY ALONE

*"And the Angel departed from her."*

1. There can be few more beautiful or more fruitful matters for contemplation than the sight and the thoughts of Mary after the Angel had "departed from her." If "there is joy before the angels of God upon one sinner that doth penance," what must have been the joy in heaven when the "fiat" of Mary had been spoken, and the gate had thereby been opened by which myriads of sinners were to enter in! The Angel departed with his message of joy, but God did not depart; that instant He began His life as man on earth, the entire possession of her whom He had chosen for His very own. Mary at that moment, the little child lost in bewildering adoration, is the joy of mankind, the joy of all the world, the joy of all the angels, the joy of God the Father, the joy of God the Son, the joy of God the Holy Spirit; and she is the joy of each individual soul that comes into the world and realizes even a little what it possesses in her.

2. What were Mary's thoughts when she came to herself, and understood what had been done? Within her own body was living the very Son of God; the Son of God was hers for ever; in a special and a very true way she could anticipate the consecrating words of the great High Priest, and of every priest that was to come

after: "This is my body—this is my blood." It was hers, and was God's free gift to her; even Mary could deserve no such honor; and therefore she would follow up her great act of faith with a jubilant act of humility: "My soul doth magnify the Lord, because He hath regarded the lowliness of His handmaiden." The Child was hers, blending into one inseparable entity a perfect saint's love of God, and a perfect mother's love of a perfect child. In such a union one can scarcely speak of joy, as one feels that joy is an inadequate term when speaking of the consummation in Heaven.

3. And on the other side saints and mystical writers have revelled in the thought of the heart of Jesus Christ when it now for the first time began to beat. They see four new relations. It found a new relation with the Father. Now for the first time can God the Son feel towards the Father, and love the Father, and serve the Father, while confined within the bondage of humanity. He now knows what it is to love, and to be unable to give that love free scope. Now for the first time God the Son has experience of human love for a human being. It knows a child's love for its mother. And now He sees human nature from the perspective of a human being: "for though He was by nature God, yet He did not set great store on His equality with God: rather, He emptied himself by taking the nature of a slave and becoming like unto men."

## THE VISITATION

Henceforth He is one with man, one with him in his littleness, one with him in his weariness; already His love is not only that of an onlooker, but of one who treads the path alongside.

### Summary

1. Mary after the Annunciation is the joy of all Heaven and earth, the one perfect thing outside of God Himself, in the truest sense "our fallen nature's solitary boast!"
2. It is easy to follow the affections of the heart of Mary at this moment, and to make them with her—faith and humility, love and adoration, etc.
3. Nor is it difficult to follow and to respond to the first affections of the Heart of Jesus when it first began to beat.

## XXI.—THE VISITATION

*"And Mary, rising up in those days, went into the hill country with haste into a city of Juda. And she entered into the house of Zachary, and saluted Elizabeth. And it came to pass that when Elizabeth heard the salutation of Mary the infant leaped in her womb. And Elizabeth was filled with the Holy Spirit, and she cried out with a loud voice and said, Blessed art thou among women, and blessed is the fruit of thy womb. And when is this to me, that the mother of my Lord should come to me? For behold as soon as the voice of thy salutation sounded in my ears, the infant in my womb leaped for joy. And blessed are thou that hast believed, because those things shall be accomplished that were spoken to thee by the Lord."—Luke i. 39-45.*

1. When Elizabeth knew of the grace of motherhood that had been conferred on her, we are told that she "hid herself five months, saying,

*THE PRINCE OF PEACE*

Thus hath the Lord dealt with me in the days wherein He hath had regard to take away my reproach among men." When Mary knew of the same grace conferred on her she, "rising up, went into the hill country with haste into a city of Juda," and there saluted Elizabeth. The spontaneous actions are significant. Elizabeth is the hermit, and cherishes the gifts of God in the contemplative life; Mary is the more active, and is prompted by the gifts of God to go and share all she has with others. Still, that she loves the contemplative soul is proved by the fact that to it she goes by preference, to it she goes "with haste," upon it she bestows the greatest blessing.

2. The fruit of the contemplative is John the Baptist; the greatest among the sons of men, "a prophet and more than a prophet," who "shall convert many of the children of Israel to the Lord their God." And so indeed it is in all time. The making of an apostle is not in the lecture-room and the public place; there he learns only the use of his weapons; they are his gymnasium. But it is in secret, in that part of his soul which answers most to the life of contemplation. The true apostle is the nearest akin to the recluse. And conversely, as is seen in Our Lady, the first work of the apostolate is charity; its first, indeed its only work.

3. The double blessing which Elizabeth has for Mary must be noted. She repeats the blessing of the Angel; the meaning of the repetition

has given room for criticism among commentators. But is it to be wondered at that the same line of thought should give rise to the same conclusion? Especially as the conclusion is so exactly fitting that it is repeated again almost immediately after by Our Lady herself, and has been spontaneously repeated ever since by all the faithful! Then she adds the further blessing: "Blessed art thou that hast believed." As if she would anticipate an answer to that question of Our Lord Himself, "Who is My mother, and who are My brethren?" He answered: "Whosoever shall do the will of My Father Who is in heaven, he is My brother, and sister, and mother." And she answers: "She who said, 'Be it done to me according to Thy word,' she, on your own showing, is indeed your Mother."

## Summary

1. In Elizabeth and in Our Lady we have types of the contemplative and apostolic natures, even as seen in active life.

2. From the contemplative comes the apostle, and back to the contemplative goes the apostle, in charity.

3. The contemplative blesses the active with a double blessing.

## XXII.—THE MAGNIFICAT

*"And Mary said: My soul doth magnify the Lord. And my spirit hath rejoiced in God my Savior."—Luke i. 46-47.*

1. Here more than anywhere else are we able to detect the soul of Our Lady; here we have

## THE PRINCE OF PEACE

her authentic biography, coming spontaneously, almost unconsciously from her lips, and in the language with which her lips are most familiar. Secondly, this hymn, as the first hymn of the New Testament, strikes the dominant note which is to ring through the rest of time and through all eternity—the note of thanksgiving which culminates in glorifying God. The note of the past had been one of endless longing; the note of the future is that of the longing satisfied. Zachary takes it up soon after; Simeon succeeds; it rings through all the writings of St. Paul; the *Gloria in excelsis* is but an expansion of the canticle; so, we may say, is the whole liturgy of the Church; so should be, but perhaps is not always, the spirit underlying every prayer of every creature of God.

2. The language in which the Magnificat is enshrined is very significant. As the Angel, when announcing the Incarnation to Our Lady, used words every one of which would recall prophecies to the mind of one familiar with them, so here, one familiar with the prophecies instinctively falls back upon them in her great thanksgiving. It is as one who in ecstacy, or in absorbed prayer, instinctively makes use of those phrases and ejaculations which linger in the mind, and which express in some way at the moment the uplifting of the heart. For the foundation of her canticle she falls back upon the canticle sung by Anna, after the birth of

# THE MAGNIFICAT

her son Samuel. For her language she recalls the constant words of prophecy. For her inspiration "her mind ranges over the whole of the dealings of God with man in the way of mercy, and over the whole of the record of those dealings as contained in the inspired books."

3. "My soul doth magnify the Lord, and my spirit hath rejoiced in God my Savior." Mary opens in the common antithetical method of Hebrew poetry, but not on that account does the second part merely repeat the meaning of the other. When she says her soul magnifies the Lord, she means that her whole being is occupied in praising, glorifying, and adoring God; when she says that her spirit rejoices in God her Jesus, she means that her spiritual understanding is turned upon the mystery of the Incarnation and Redemption, and all it has meant and means to her, and that the understanding has flooded her with intense light and joy. "To magnify the Lord is to form the highest and largest conceptions of His greatness and goodness, to form those conceptions into the shape of mental and most heartfelt praise in whatever way is open to the heart or soul."

## Summary

1. Mary reveals her soul most of all in the Magnificat. In it she strikes the note for the music of all future ages: thanksgiving and glory to God.

2. She takes as her plan the canticle of Anna; she finds her language in the prophets; her inspiration

*THE PRINCE OF PEACE*

is the goodness of God to man; in all she shows where her mind has always dwelt.

3. Her whole being is engaged in praising God; her understanding of the Savior is an ocean of joy to her.

## XXIII.—THE MAGNIFICAT (continued)

*"Because He hath regarded the humility of His handmaid, for behold from henceforth all generations shall call me blessed. For He that is mighty hath done great things to me, and holy is His name. And His mercy is from generation unto generation to them that fear him."—Luke i. 48-50.*

1. By "humility" the original Greek here intends not the virtue of humility, which is in itself a great grace of God, and it usually ill becomes its possessor to proclaim it, but rather her actual lowliness, her poverty, her insignificance, her obscurity, her low and poor estate, her worthlessness as in her own eyes it appeared. She makes a contrast in this second sentence between herself and God—He the Lord, she the handmaiden; He the great, she the tiny! He the generous Lover who chooses her, she the chosen who can only make return by devotedness to her Lord.

2. "Behold from henceforth all generations shall call me Blessed." The tiny maiden, who knows nothing better than her own littleness, glories in the thought that for all time her name will stand for a symbol of the great goodness of God to man, that this symbol will grow

*THE MAGNIFICAT*

more and more significant, and that the more significant it grows, and the more she is honored, so much the more will her Lord be glorified. As some beautiful picture or work of art by being honored brings honor to its maker, and the more it is honored the more is its maker glorified, so does Our Lady, the masterpiece of the hand of God in this creation, gather up in all generations ever more glory to God. The Angel Gabriel began the song of glory: "Blessed art thou among women"; St. Elizabeth took it up: "Blessed art thou among women"; St. Peter must have known what was implied when he said: "Thou art Christ the Son of the living God"; and the heart of every woman finds expression in that poor woman's voice from the crowd: "Blessed is the womb that bore Thee, and the breasts that gave Thee suck."

3. Having bowed down before her Lord, and having risen up in exultation and thanksgiving, Mary now sets herself to detail the goodness and greatness of her Lord. "He hath done great things to me," she cries, for the Hebrew bears this rendering, "He who is mighty, He Whose name is holy, He Whose mercy is from generation unto generation, to them that fear Him." His power, His holiness, His mercy, are the three attributes she chooses; His power, in the wonderful fact and manner of the Incarnation; His holiness, in the person of Him Who has become incarnate, in the manner of the Incar-

nation, in its object, in the work which it will accomplish, in the fruits it will produce for earth and heaven; His mercy, because the Incarnation was the great work of restoration, of reconciliation, of atonement, of satisfaction, of infinite condescension and compassion.

### Summary

1. "He hath regarded the humility of His handmaid." Mary contrasts her own material and actual littleness with the greatness of her Lord.
2. "From henceforth all generations shall call me blessed." Mary dwells on the thought of the glory that is to come to her Lord because of all He has done for her.
3. She then extols the three great attributes of God displayed in the Incarnation: His mighty power, His holy name, His mercy.

### XXIV.—THE MAGNIFICAT (continued)

*"He hath showed might in His arm; He hath scattered the proud in the conceit of their hearts. He hath put down the mighty from their seat and hath exalted the humble. He hath filled the hungry with good things, and the rich He hath sent empty away."—Luke i. 51-53.*

1. Here more than ever does one hear in Mary's words an echo of the Old Testament. She seems again to be linking up the past with the future; the past with its constant record of the proud being brought low, and the lowly and crushed being again restored: and the future, still more explicitly portrayed in the

## THE MAGNIFICAT

thanksgiving prayer of our Lord: "I thank thee, Father, Lord of heaven and earth, that Thou hast hidden these things from the wise and prudent, and hast revealed them unto little ones." And again by St. Paul: "The weak things of this world hath God chosen to confound the strong, that no flesh may glory in his sight."

2. But above all, these words, like the rest of the Magnificat, must be specially referred to the Incarnation. It is as if Our Lady said: "By the Incarnation God hath shown His might, by it He has scattered the proud. By it He hath put down the mighty, by it He hath exalted the humble," etc. And St. Paul applies this with even greater point, first to our Lord Himself, and then by imitation to all Christianity, when he says: "Let this mind be in you which was also in Christ Jesus, who being in the form of God thought it not robbery to be equal with God, but emptied Himself taking the form of a servant, being made in the likeness of man and in habit found as man. He humbled Himself, becoming obedient unto death, even to the death of the cross. For which cause God also hath exalted Him, and hath given Him a name which is above all names, that at the name of Jesus every knee should bow, of those that are in heaven, on earth, and under the earth, and that every tongue should confess that the Lord Jesus is in the glory of God the Father."

3. In the first of these three verses Our Lady

# THE PRINCE OF PEACE

does but speak of the victory of the Incarnation over evil. In the second she repeats that proclamation of victory, and then of its championing of the lowly. In the third she speaks of the positive good the Incarnation does, and this she now puts in the first place. "He hath filled the hungry with good things." The hungering past is now satisfied; hungry nature has now found what it wants. She anticipates the blessings of the Beatitudes: "Blessed are the poor in spirit, Blessed are they that hunger and thirst after justice," etc. She anticipates the constant cries and promises of our Lord: "Come to me all you that labor and are burdened, and I will refresh you." "He that is thirsty, let him come to me and drink," and last, and greatest of all, she foreshadows that great fruit of the Incarnation, the Blessed Sacrament: "My body is meat indeed, and My blood is drink indeed. He that eateth My flesh and drinketh my blood abideth in Me and I in him." Indeed God "hath filled the hungry with good things" by means of the Incarnation!

## Summary

1. "He hath showed might in His arm," etc. "The weak things of this world hath God chosen to confound the strong."

2. "He hath put down the mighty," etc. And hath exalted the humble, above all the self-humbled Jesus Christ, and whoever will follow Him.

3. "He hath filled the hungry with good things," etc.—the hungry past, hungry nature, the hungry future, above all those who hunger for Christ Incarnate.

## THE MAGNIFICAT

### XXV.—THE MAGNIFICAT (continued)

*"He hath received Israel His servant, being mindful of His mercy. As He spoke to our fathers, to Abraham and to his seed for ever. And Mary abode with her about three months, and she returned to her own house."—Luke i. 54-56.*

1. At the close of the canticle Mary again very emphatically reveals to us the material source of all her inspiration. She has always dwelt upon the past. She has watched the continued faithfulness and mercy of God, "ruling from end to end mightily, and disposing all things sweetly," making "all things co-operate to good for those who love Him," even though "His ways are not our ways," and it is only afterwards, when everything is seen in its right perspective, that the great truth of His tenderhearted goodness guiding all is brought home to us. Mary sees all in this perspective; how at the beginning God "received"—*i.e.*, "chose," "took hold of," the people of Israel, her words echoing those of Isaias: "But thou Israel, art my servant, Jacob, whom I have chosen, the seed of Abraham my friend," and handing on the contemplation to St. Paul, who says: "Nowhere doth He take hold of the angels, but of the seed of Abraham he taketh hold."

2. "As He spoke to our fathers." Mary's vision is that of the student as well as of the saint. God could, she tells herself, have done otherwise. He could have brought about the

redemption by other ways than this, less humiliating to the Son of God. But He has chosen this means, and having chosen it, nothing in the world shall make Him change—not the dejection, repeated and repeated, of His own people, not the faithlessness of individuals, generation after generation. Whatever else God seems to be with man, behind all the seeming He has proved again and again that His promises are sure, His word is true; and in return He does but ask that man should believe and hope. Mary sees well enough the tottering of this world. She sees the tottering of man upon its heaving surface. She sees the hand held out from the skies to hold man up. And she reminds man that that hand has never failed anyone who has grasped it.

3. Thus the Magnificat sums up, in a great outburst of thanksgiving, man's history in the past and man's history in the future, and centers it all upon the Incarnation, and upon her whom "all generations shall call blessed." It describes to us the ways of God's dealings with man, which are not as man's ways, by means of lowliness, by elevation of the down-trodden, not by the means of which man makes most account. The Church takes up the song; she sings it in her Office every evening throughout the year; reminding herself and her children of this glorious aspect of the world's history, and of her by whom this aspect has been made known. And in it she sees the record of her

## THE BIRTH OF ST. JOHN

own ultimate triumph; not merely at the end of all, but in each succeeding day she knows that in her lowliness, by her suppression, through her very hungering after justice, the work of God is being done.

### Summary

1. "He hath received Israel his servant, being mindful of His mercy." Mary dwells at the end on the perfect faithfulness of God, which is the greatest fruit of His mercy.

2. In that faithfulness, proved beyond any doubt to one who sees aright, she sees the basis of endless confidence under all circumstances, in all times.

3. The Church accepts the message and repeats it every day, for herself and for every individual. "God is faithful," says St. Paul, "who will not suffer us to be tempted beyond that which we are able."

## XXVI.—THE BIRTH OF ST. JOHN

*"Now Elizabeth's full time of being delivered was come, and she brought forth a son. And her neighbors and kinsfolk heard that the Lord had showed His great mercy towards her, and they congratulated with her. And it came to pass that on the eighth day they came to circumcise the child, and they called him by his father's name, Zachary. And his mother, answering, said, Not so, but he shall be called John. And they said to her, There is none of thy kindred that is called by this name. And they made signs to his father how he would have him called. And demanding a writing-table, he wrote, saying: John is his name. And they wondered. And immediately his mouth was opened, and his tongue was loosed, and he spoke blessing God. And fear came upon all their neighbors, and all these things were noised abroad over all the hill country of Judea, and all they that had heard them laid them up in their heart, saying,*

## THE PRINCE OF PEACE

*What a one, think ye, shall this child be? For the hand of the Lord was with him."—Luke i. 57-66.*

1. This is one of those scenes in the Gospel which are full of mystery to us modern believers, because, as it were, it seems to put before us the direct interference of God with the things of this world. In the first age "God walked with Adam," and brought him the animals that he might name them. In this age of Elizabeth and Zachary and Mary He walked with them by means of His Angels, and still, in such special cases as these, insisted that the name to be given should not be meaningless. With us, so it seems to us, He permits things to take their course; our names have no meaning in themselves, they are only given to distinguish us. And so in other matters He does not seem to interfere. None the less is He faithful. If we have not signs such as these, we have signs that are greater—the miracle of the Church, the Blessed Sacrament, the constant wonder-working of grace.

2. But with John, as with our Lord Himself, and as with no other in the New Testament that we know, God interfered that the significant name should be given. "John is his name," the "mercy" or the "grace of God," as the Angel had told to Zachary. One can look on with wonder, as did the neighbors, at this insistence on the name; but when we realize all that John the Baptist is to represent, one need not be

## THE BIRTH OF ST. JOHN

surprised. John is the last of the long line of prophets sent to lift up the people in their depression and in their fall. He is to be the great source of grace for the generation in which he is to live. He is to be the preacher of still greater graces to come. He is to show the way to those graces: "Do penance, for the Kingdom of God is at hand."

3. There is something triumphantly joyful about this birth of St. John the Baptist. The joy of the mother, who had been blessed with the child in her old age; of the father, whose "tongue was loosed, and he spoke, blessing God"; of the gathered crowd, who "wondered" and "feared" with that joyful fear of which the Gospels often speak; of the child himself, who had "leapt in the womb" at the coming of our Lord; all this is at first in marked contrast with that mortified, austere, denouncing figure which we generally associate with the name of the Baptist. But those who understand know that the two are not antagonistic; that austerity and joy go hand in hand; and the Italian artists who are so fond of painting the child John playing happily with the Child Jesus at Mary's knee, obey a true spiritual instinct.

### Summary
1. The wonderful hand of God, at times manifest, at other times hidden, but always there.
2. The significance of the name of John.
3. John the union of great joy and austerity.

## XXVII.—THE BENEDICTUS

*"And Zachary his father was filled with the Holy Spirit, and he prophesied, saying, Blessed be the Lord God of Israel, because He hath visited and wrought the redemption of His people, and He hath raised up a horn of salvation for us in the house of David his servant. As he spoke by the mouth of his holy prophets who are from the beginning, salvation from our enemies, and from the hand of all that hate us. To perform mercy to our fathers, and to remember his holy testament, the oath which he swore to Abraham our father that he would grant us. That being delivered from the hand of our enemies we may serve him without fear, in holiness and justice before him all our days."—Luke i. 67-75.*

1. Like the canticle of Mary, the canticle of Zachary is full of Old Testament echoes, and it begins where the former ends. Mary closed with the record of the faithfulness of God, Zachary makes this the keynote of this first part of the Benedictus. The Lord has visited, has come to His people, as He had promised that He would; He has "received Israel His servant, being mindful of His mercy"; "With the Lord there is mercy and with Him plentiful redemption," as the Psalmist has sung; he understands, as Mary has understood, the wide significance of the prophecies of old, reaching beyond the chosen people, to the wide boundaries of the Kingdom of Jesus Christ. It is this note of the Kingdom mentioned by the Angel at the Annunciation which Zachary adds to the Magnificat.

2. Then he draws from the prophets two notes

## THE BENEDICTUS

by which the Kingdom shall be known. The first is "salvation from our enemies," the first characteristic of a stable kingdom; that characteristic promptly promised by our Lord when He founded it on Peter: "Thou art Peter, and upon this rock I will build my Church, and the gates of hell shall not prevail against it." And how wonderfully the promise is fulfilled! For while the enemies, internal and external, both "flesh and blood," as St. Paul calls them, and "principalities and powers," seem to be for ever triumphant, the Kingdom is for ever making greater conquests. And here the singer adds a parenthesis, a kind of play upon three names; for "the name of John signifies the grace or mercy of God, the name of Zachary signifies the memory of God, the name of Elizabeth signifies the oath of God."

3. The second characteristic of a stable kingdom is "internal peace and wealth and security, in the abundant means and resources of the citizens, their mutual harmony, their obedience to the laws, their freedom from everything that may breed division, disturbance, discontent." And this Zachary gives as the second note of the new Kingdom when he says: "That being delivered from the hand of our enemies we may serve Him without fear, in holiness and justice before Him all our days." As St. Paul in his own way puts it, contrasting the security of the new law with the encumbrances of the old:

"You have not received the spirit of bondage again in fear, but you have received the spirit of adoption of sons whereby we cry, Abba, Father." Service of love and not of fear, holiness and justice abiding, these are the characteristics of the new Kingdom.

### Summary

1. The Benedictus takes up the praise of the faithfulness of God, with which the Magnificat concluded.
2. It goes on to dwell on the new Kingdom and its characteristics; first, security from without.
3. Second, peace, security, and therefore service of love within.

## XXVIII.—THE BENEDICTUS (continued)

*"And thou, child, shalt be called the prophet of the Highest, for thou shalt go before the face of the Lord to prepare His way. To give knowledge of salvation to His people unto the remission of their sins. Through the bowels of the mercy of our God, in which the orient from on high hath visited us. To enlighten them that sit in darkness, and in the shadow of death, to direct our feet into the way of peace. And the child grew, and was strengthened in spirit, and was in the desert until the day of his manifestation to Israel."—Luke i. 76-80.*

1. The first part of the Benedictus develops the last part of the Magnificat; this second part develops the words of the Angel Gabriel to Zachary: "He shall go before him in the spirit and power of Elias, that he may turn the hearts of the fathers unto the children, and the in-

## THE BENEDICTUS

credulous to the wisdom of the just, to prepare unto the Lord a perfect people." John was to be the forerunner of our Lord; he was to prepare it by means of penance; and when he had prepared it he was to point out to men our Lord Himself among them. Though apparently he was to work no miracle, though he was to make no striking prophecy, he was to be "a prophet and more than a prophet," on the testimony of our Lord Himself; it was enough that he was to show the people the way to the remission of their sins by means of that salvation, that Savior, the Lamb of God, Who was among them. St. John is the ideal apostle.

2. "Through the bowels of the mercy of God." In these last verses Zachary shows how much he belongs to the spirit of the new law. He recognizes the sin of man; he sees their remission in the Savior Jesus Christ; he recognizes that this remission is nothing of right, but is a pure condescension of God; he concludes, with tears in his uplifted eyes, that this condescension can be prompted by nothing but mercy and love; he anticipates in his own gentle way the cry of St. Paul: "Christ loved me, and gave Himself for me." "God might have had mercy in a thousand ways. But the way He has chosen was the way of this visitation, for love is not content with mercy. It must itself share the low condition of those it loves, and this has issued in God becoming Man." The old man is over-

whelmed with the thought that has grown upon him in these three months, and well may the thought overwhelm us all.

3. "And the child grew, and was strengthened in spirit, and was in the deserts until the day of his manifestation unto Israel." This is all we are told of the training of St. John. But it is not nothing; above all it tells us one thing. He was "in the desert." So our Lord Himself went into the desert. So St. Paul retired into the desert. The desert, it is abundantly proved, is the best school for the apostolate. We peer into the darkness and discover St. John, in prayer, in mortification, in self-suppression, forcing his way, as it were, through the valley of this death into the presence of God! in that presence learning things which it is not given to man to express; from that presence looking back on mankind, and thereby understanding with a depth that passes man's own comprehension. So does an apostle gain all by losing all, live by death, confound the strong by his own worldly weakness.

## Summary

1. The mission of John was that of the ideal apostle; to prepare man, and to lead him to Jesus Christ, through contrition and penance.

2. Thence in the study of Jesus Christ we discover the motive of His condescension, which is that of pure love.

3. And John was himself to learn these things, both his mission and man to whom he was to be sent, by life alone in the wilderness.

## XXIX.—THE TRIAL OF ST. JOSEPH

*"Now the generation of Christ was in this wise. When as his Mother Mary was espoused to Joseph, before they came together, she was found with child, of the Holy Spirit. Whereupon Joseph her husband, being a just man, and not willing publicly to expose her, was minded to put her away privately. But while he thought on these things, behold the Angel of the Lord appeared to him in sleep, saying, Joseph, son of David, fear not to take unto thee Mary thy wife, for that which is conceived of her is of the Holy Spirit. And she shall bring forth a Son, and thou shalt call His name Jesus. For He shall save the people from their sins.... And Joseph, rising up from sleep, did as the Angel of the Lord had commanded him, and took unto him his wife."*—Matt. i. 18-25.

1. It is natural, almost inevitable, for us to wonder where St. Joseph had been all this time, and what part he had been called upon to play in the work of these nine months. That Mary should have been able to tell him was impossible; even Mary's word could not have been evidence enough for an event so eminently supernatural. Nevertheless, her word would have been a sufficient guarantee of her own innocence; hence that Joseph could ever have suspected Mary of infidelity is obviously impossible. But that must have made his own position all the more difficult. Mary was with child, and Mary was the most perfect creature he knew. But to be with child implied a father; and it was not himself. There seemed but one solution; he had no right to the

*THE PRINCE OF PEACE*

Child, therefore he had no right to the Mother. His judgment went no farther.

2. On the other hand one may reasonably suppose in St. Joseph at least as much understanding of the Scriptures and of the promised Messiah as was found among the faithful Jews of his time. He knew what the priests knew, that the time was at hand; he knew that the Child was to be of the House of David, his own house and that of Mary; he knew that the prophecies included a virgin mother, Bethlehem, and Nazareth; he knew as much, perhaps, as Zachary knew, or Simeon, or Anna the prophetess. This was all on the positive side. But it did not solve his problem. He did not recognize any right of his own to interfere in a thing so sacred. If God had chosen Mary, and had given her this Child for her own, he had not yet evidence that he too had been chosen. If God had chosen her, God would look to her in His own way. Whatever else we know of Joseph, we know this, that he trusted God to work out His own ends.

3. At length came the answer, and it came in the manner consistent with all the rest of God's dealings with Joseph. God might have told him at the outset, and so have freed him from this anxiety; just as later He might have sent him earlier to Bethlehem, and so have found a more becoming dwelling-place in which the Child should be born; as He might have given him

## THE EXPECTATION

longer warning before hurrying him off to Egypt; as He might have instructed him about his abode on his return; as He might have told him about the staying of the Child in Jerusalem, at the time that He was lost. But that was not God's way with Joseph, as it is not His way with most of us. This world is a trial ground; and not the least of our trials are the problems which we have continually to face and solve. In this Joseph is our model.

### Summary

1. The cause of the doubt to Joseph: what he did not know.
2. The evidence on the other side: what St. Joseph did know.
3. The consistency of this treatment of Joseph with the rest of his life.

### XXX.—THE EXPECTATION

*"Be comforted, be comforted My people, saith your God. Speak ye to the heart of Jerusalem, and call to her: for her evil is come to an end, her iniquity is forgiven: she hath received of the hand of the Lord double for her sins. The voice of one crying in the desert: Prepare ye the way of the Lord, make straight in the wilderness the paths of our God. Every valley shall be exalted, and every mountain shall be laid low, and the crooked shall become straight, and the rough ways plain. And the glory of the Lord shall be revealed and all flesh together shall see that the mouth of the Lord hath spoken."*
—Isa. xl. 1-5.

1. For six months Mary was alone in Nazareth awaiting the birth of her Son. It is not difficult to imagine some at least of her thoughts

during that half-year. (1) She realized more and more what a stupendous act had been accomplished, that God, Who lived always in His own creation, had now come to live in it in a new and special way; (2) that this could not but mean for all mankind a new and special source of grace and union with its God; (3) that she had been chosen as the special means for this union, and for this communication of graces; (4) that this was but the beginning of God's new favors to men, what would be afterwards no one could fathom; (5) that all this was the outcome of love.

2. Then there was the intense longing, the very agony of waiting. All nature had been groaning through the centuries for this manifestation, and had not known why. All the pagan world had become sick to death waiting for this "unknown God" Who would put an end to all their false worship. The chosen people had, many of them, grown weary with the delay, and had fainted on the roadside; the faithful among them had made "How long, O Lord, how long?" their constant prayer. Then we can well understand, though we cannot comprehend, the longing of Our Lady as she counted the months, the weeks and the days before her Son would be given to the world. And that longing was intensified by the fact that she was to be His Mother—a fact which, perhaps, only a mother can rightly understand. "If our Lord's presence

## THE EXPECTATION

in the womb had made the unborn Baptist leap for joy, what must have been the desire of Mary to take her own Child into her arms and press Him to her heart?"

3. And along with all this was the constant wonder how it was all to come about. He was to be born in Bethlehem; yet so far there was no prospect of this. It was to be God's doing; therefore they would not take it upon themselves to interpret the prophecies. Suddenly the moment came; and, as always, emperors and kings were made to fulfil the will of God; the empire of Rome was made to "prepare the way of the Lord," to "make straight the path for our Lord," to send out its orders so that Mary might be brought to Bethlehem, and that her Son might be born in the circumstances that most became Him. We watch them on the journey, Mary and Joseph; their hardships and their gaiety of heart, their sorrows and their joys, their submission and their triumph, their weakness and their glory; while the Child Whom they bear with them longs for the moment when He, too, may begin His task of winning man by love.

### Summary

1. The many thoughts, and following on them the many acts of the heart of our Lady during her six months of waiting.

2. Above all her great longing, being as it was the crowning longing felt in all Creation.

3. The way God commands the world to serve Him; and the sight of Mary and Joseph on their journey to Bethlehem.

# PART II
# *CHRISTMAS*

## I.—THE NATIVITY

*"And it came to pass that in those days there went out a decree from Caesar Augustus, that the whole world should be enrolled. This enrolling was first done by Cyrinus, the governor of Syria. And all went to be enrolled, every one into his own city. And Joseph also went up from Galilee out of the city of Nazareth into Judea, to the city of David, which is called Bethlehem, because he was of the house and family of David, to be enrolled with Mary his espoused wife, who was with child. And it came to pass that when they were there her days were accomplished that she should be delivered. And she brought forth her first-born Son, and wrapped Him up in swaddling-clothes, and laid Him in a manger, because there was no room for them in the inn."*
—*Luke ii. 1-7.*

1. It is characteristic of the Gospels that the greatest events are told in the fewest words and with the utmost simplicity. The institution of the Blessed Sacrament, the Crucifixion, the power of Absolution, are all told in a sentence; and the story of the birth of our Lord is no exception to the rule. Indeed, but for St. Luke we might not have heard of it at all. But per-

## THE NATIVITY

haps we have enough. To begin with we know that "there was no room for them in the inn." Nor, apparently, was there much room for them in all Bethlehem. Nor, later was there room for them in all Palestine. Nor, later still, does there seem to be much room for Him in all the world. Nor today is there much room for Him in the lives and hearts of most men. But I must not blame others; is there much room for Him in mine?

2. Still a shelter of some kind was found, though it is to be noticed that St. Luke does not mention it. If we had no more than his description to go upon, we should almost be compelled to conclude that our Lord was born in the gutter by the roadside; literally the birth of a pauper and an outcast. The mention of the manger leads us to conclude that there was a shelter of some sort overhead; but not all mangers are indoors, especially in the East. Still let us accept the firm tradition, for the sake of our pitiful human nature if for nothing else; when our King first came into this world, at least He was given a stable cave in which He could be born, at least He was treated as well as our cattle, if not as well as ourselves.

3. And now that He is born, and lies helpless and apparently unnoticing before us like any other infant, let us kneel beside Him, with Mary, and Joseph, and the maid, and the countless saints who from that time till today have found

in the mere sight of this Child enough to satisfy all their strongest cravings. Let us watch Him and his first adorers, in company with St. Gertrude, and St. Bridget, and St. Theresa. Let us take Him into our arms and nurse Him, as St. Bonaventure recommends us, and as St. Anthony of Padua was privileged to do, and St. Stanislaus Kostka, and so many more saints of weary life and labor. Let us give Him back to Our Lady, and learn from her a lesson on the way her Child should be treated. Let us hear the words ringing round the room, for our own greater consolation: "As many as received Him, to them he gave power to become the sons of God, to them that believe in His name." "Brethren," comments St. John on his own words, "you are now sons of God, but you know not what you shall be."

*Summary*

1. "There was no room for Him in the inn." Nor has there been much room for Him anywhere in this world.
2. "He was laid in a manger." At least this much was given Him; and it is enough to satisfy Him.
3. It is much for us to be able to unite ourselves with His first adorers.

## II.—THE NATIVITY (continued)

*"And thou, Bethlehem Ephrata, art a little one among the thousands of Juda: out of thee shall He come forth unto me that is to be the ruler in Israel; and His going forth is from the beginning, from the*

## THE NATIVITY

*days of eternity.... And He shall stand, and feed in the strength of the Lord, in the height of the name of the Lord His God: and they shall be converted, for now shall He be magnified even to the ends of the earth."*—Mic. v. 2-4.

1. In meditating on the Child in the manger we cannot do better than follow the meditations of His own saints. First is that of St. Paul; this is how his thoughts go: "Let that mind be in you which was also in Christ Jesus. For He, though He was by nature God, yet did not set great store on His equality with God; rather, He emptied Himself by taking the nature of a slave and becoming like unto men. And after He had appeared in outward form as man, He humbled Himself [yet more] by obedience, yea, unto death upon a cross. Wherefore God hath exalted Him above the highest, and hath bestowed on Him the name which is above every name; that at the name of Jesus every knee should bend in heaven, on earth, and under the earth, and that every tongue should confess that Jesus Christ is Lord, to the glory of God the Father" (Phil. ii. 5-11, Westminster version). Thus St. Paul dwells upon the Nativity in its reference to our Lord Himself, His humiliation in it, and His glory.

2. Next is St. John, writing long after St. Paul. He says "The Word was made flesh, and dwelt among us (and we saw his glory, the glory as it were of the only begotten of the

Father), full of grace and truth.... And of His fulness we all have received, and grace for grace. For the law was given by Moses, grace and truth by Jesus Christ. No man hath seen God at any time; the only begotten Son Who is in the bosom of the Father, He hath declared Him" (John i. 14-18). And he comments on this passage in these words: "By this hath the love of God appeared to us, because God hath sent His only begotten Son into the world, that we may live by Him. In this is love: not as though we had loved God, but because He hath first loved us, and sent His Son to be a propitiation for our sins. My dearest, if God hath so loved us; we also ought to love one another" (1 John iv. 9-11). Thus St. John dwells upon the Nativity in its reference to us.

3. Yet a further contemplation is that of St. Ignatius Loyola. He bids us "to see and consider what they are doing—that is to say, the journey and the labor that they undergo in order that our Lord may be born in extreme poverty; and in order that after such toils, after hunger, thirst, heat, cold, insults, and affronts, He may die on the Cross, and all this for me; and then by reflecting to derive some spiritual profit." Thus does the saint apply to this meditation his principle that "love ought to be found in deeds rather than in words"; and by dwelling on the deeds of love of Christ our Lord, begun here in the manger of Bethlehem, he would

stir us to like deeds of love in our degree; how, as he says elsewhere, "I on my side, with great reason and justice, ought to offer and give to His Divine Majesty all things that are mine, and myself with them."

### Summary

1. St. Paul dwells on the example of humiliation contained in the Nativity, and exhorts us to follow.
2. St. John dwells on the example of love, and exhorts us to the same.
3. St. Ignatius dwells on the example of sacrifice, the truest test of love: "all this for me."

## III.—THE ANGELS AND THE SHEPHERDS

*"And there were in the same country shepherds watching and keeping the night-watches over their flocks. And behold an Angel of the Lord stood by them, and the brightness of God shone about them, and they feared with a great fear. And the Angel said to them, Fear not, for behold I bring you tidings of great joy, that shall be to all the people: for this day is born to you a Savior, who is Christ the Lord, in the city of David. And this shall be a sign to you: you shall find the infant wrapped in swaddling-clothes, and laid in a manger."—Luke ii. 8-12.*

1. Later in His life, when our Lord was preaching on the Kingdom of Heaven, he described the master of the feast as angry with those who had been invited and had refused, and as giving orders that his servants should turn to those in the by-ways, and should compel them to come in. Such indeed has been His

way from the beginning until now: "the poor have the Gospel preached to them"; in the poor rests the true life of the Church; a safe test of the power of the Church in any country is the hold she has upon the poor of that country. And this character of His call was the first He struck on coming into the world. The great and powerful had ignored Him; the busy world had all manner of excuses; so His angels were sent to the shepherds on the hill-side, here, as so often afterwards, the first-fruits of His coming.

2. Nor is it to be by some kind of accident that these shepherds are to be called. They are not to wander down the hill and along the road to Bethlehem, and to find the Child on the way. It is possible that the cave was one in which they had often taken shelter; but that was not to be their guide this night. Another principle God would establish; not only would He show that the poor are His special choice, but He would also show that, when He willed it, He is independent of man for the spreading of His glory. He has His ministering angels, sometimes manifesting themselves to simple souls, more often doing their work in hiddenness, because the souls of men are not simple. It is a true instinct which makes us associate angels with little children; for it is the eyes of simple children that best can see them; it is the minds of children that best can understand them, just as it is little children that seem to come nearest

## THE ANGELS AND THE SHEPHERDS

to grasping the reality of the Blessed Sacrament.

3. The shepherds "feared with a great fear" at the sight of the Angel of the Lord who stood by them, and at the brightness of God which shone about them; as who would not? But this implies no doubt; it implies the simplicity of children. So they were reassured; and as children they accepted the reassurance. "Fear not," said the Angel; this is the third time we have heard the words from an angel's lips. "Fear not, Mary," Our Lady was told; "Fear not, Zachary," was said to the priest; and now "Fear not" is said to the shepherds and "all the people." No wonder that a master-saint has said that the first operation of an angel of light is to calm the human soul and to remove from it fear and unrest. The rest of his message is full of deep meaning. He brings "tidings of great joy, which shall be to all the people." The message is the news of the birth of the "Savior, Who is Christ the Lord." And they are shown how and when they shall find Him. And to this day Christmas remains the season of "great joy to all the people."

### Summary

1. The shepherds are the first called to the Crib; consistently with the rest of Our Lord's practice.
2. They are called by the Angel; in great moments God acts independently of men.
3. The message is one of great joy; which has been "to all the people" from that day to this.

## IV.—THE ANGELS' SONG

*"And suddenly there was with the Angel a multitude of the Heavenly host, praising God and saying, Glory to God in the highest, and on earth peace to men of goodwill."—Luke ii. 13-14.*

1. It was fitting that this manifestation of the angels should have been made on this night of the Nativity. The fathers of the Church, when speaking of the fall of the rebel angels, tend to explain it as the refusal to adore the Incarnate God that was to be; they would not bow down before Him who was to make Himself "less than the angels." Hence, when the actual manifestation came, those who had been faithful could not but have rejoiced; they must have seen in that Child more than even Mary saw, for they saw His Godhead shining through His human frame, and they recognized in Him the great union of God with men. Later our Lord was to speak of His own love for and reliance on His angels; in the entrusting to them of children, in the use He would make of them to separate the just from the unjust, in the acceptance of an angel to strengthen Him in the Garden of Gethsemane; in the knowledge that He had but to ask His Father and legions of angels would come to His support. Christmas Day, then, is a feast of the angels as well as of men.

2. "Glory to God in the highest, and on earth peace to men of goodwill." This was the angels'

## THE ANGELS' SONG

song of praise. It has two divisions. First, at the moment of our Lord's great humiliation on this earth, the angels break out with their chorus of praise. St. Paul saw it in the same light: "He hath humbled Himself...therefore God hath exalted Him." Then the consequences to war-worn man are recorded. Man at war with God, man at war with himself, man all restless, is at last to be given peace, if only he will have it. Again St. Paul sees with the angels' eyes: "He is our peace," he says, "Who hath made both one, and breaking down the middle wall of partition, the enmities, in His flesh, making void the law of commandments contained in decrees, that He might make the two in Himself into one man, making peace, and might reconcile both to God in one body on the cross, killing the enmities in Himself.." It was not merely the "Pax Romana," at that moment reigning, that the angels announced; it was the still greater "Peace which the world cannot give," which those alone know who possess it.

3. The Church has taken these words of the angels and has built upon them one of the most beautiful of her hymns. In the first part she dwells on and expands the first words of the angels, endeavoring to give expression to their affections when she sings: *Laudamus te, benedicimus te, adoramus te, glorificamus te. Gratias agimus tibi propter magnam gloriam tuam.* Then the hymn turns to the earthly results of the

great mystery, hailing our Lord as the Incarnate Son, the Lamb of God, who brings about peace on earth by means of the redemption in His blood. This is God the Man, the Redeemer, Who taketh away the sins of the world. And, lastly, He is called upon as having accomplished His work and reigning in heaven, where He is associated with the Father and the Holy Spirit: *Domine Fili unigenite, Jesu Christe. Domine Deus, Agnus Dei, Filius Patris. Qui tollis peccata mundi, miserere nobis. Qui tollis peccata mundi, suscipe deprecationem nostram. Quoniam tu solus sanctus, tu solus Dominus, tu solus altissimus, Jesu Christe, cum Sancto Spiritu in gloria Dei Patris.*

## Summary

1. The fitness of the adoration of the Angels at the Nativity.
2. The fitness of their song: Glory to God, peace to men of goodwill.
3. The development of this by the Church.

## V.—THE ADORATION OF THE SHEPHERDS

*"And it came to pass that after the Angels departed from them into Heaven the shepherds said one to another, let us go over to Bethlehem, and let us see this word that is come to pass, which the Lord hath showed to us. And they came with haste, and they found Mary and Joseph, and the Infant lying in a manger. And seeing, they understood of the word that had been spoken to them concerning the Child. And all they that heard wondered, and at those things that were told them by the shepherds.*

## THE ADORATION OF THE SHEPHERDS

*But Mary kept all these words, pondering them in her heart. And the shepherds returned, glorifying and praising God, for all the things they had heard and seen, as it was told unto them."—Luke ii. 15-20.*

1. Christian simplicity loves most to dwell on this visit of the shepherds to the manger. It is pictured more than any other scene; our cribs always try to represent it; our Christmas hymns, especially our oldest carols, win us with the simple story. And the reason is not difficult to find; for the shepherds "coming with haste," without any express injunction from the angels, without any shadow of doubt in their hearts, and finding, apparently so easily, "Mary and Joseph and the Infant," and "understanding of the word," though what they exactly "understood" they probably could not have told us—all this is eminently typical of that spirit of devotion which runs through all Christianity, which makes children "understand" the Blessed Sacrament, and which "draws all things to Himself," the hearts of men finding in Christ our Lord the peace and the certainty which are nowhere else.

2. The shepherds went away happy men. They had not known happiness of this kind before. They could not have wished to be anything other than just what they were; they would not have exchanged their rank with anyone; even now, wherever they are in heaven, one may safely say with St. Luke they are "glorifying and

## THE PRINCE OF PEACE

praising God for all the things they had heard and seen, as it had been told them" that night. So often in our lives there are moments which have made all the rest of life worth living, and for which we shall never cease to praise God for all eternity—a conversion, a special grace through the sacraments, a special light which has made us understand, a crisis through which we have been guided, a vocation, a dedication in some peculiar way, a proof beyond possibility of doubt of our Lord's favor, and protection, and guidance, and intense love. We owe our Lord very much; we thank Him very little; the shepherds remind us of this duty.

3. There were two sets of people affected by the shepherds. The first were the simple people who heard the simple story from their simple lips. "And all they that heard wondered at these things that were told them by the shepherds." There was proof enough for them in the narrative itself and in those who told it; just as little Bernadette is proof enough in herself of the Lourdes apparitions, or as a child that pours out its little heart in its first communion is proof enough in its degree of the Blessed Sacrament. They wondered; they did not pretend to understand; they were content to revere. And, secondly, there was Our Lady. "But Mary kept all these words, pondering them in her heart." How did she "ponder" them? What were her reflections? What deepest

*OUR LADY'S ADORATION*

thoughts of deepest poets could compare with Our Lady's ponderings? She knew so much, yet so little; and the much that she knew made her lose herself in God's infinity.

*Summary*

1. The shepherds the models of devotion.
2. The effects of devotion on themselves.
3. Their effect on others.

## VI.—OUR LADY'S ADORATION

*"But Mary kept all these words, pondering them in her heart."*—Luke ii. 19.

1. We are more than justified in thinking that this sentence, repeated elsewhere of Our Lady by St. Luke, is intended to tell us something peculiarly characteristic of her. "It seems as if they were meant to imply that she was especially one of those souls whose great book from which they learn is the daily providence of God, the course of His dealings with them in their own lives, and in the incidents which come across them therein. Such souls need no other lessons than those which are thus given them day after day, and they find in them most abundant instruction as to the very highest secrets and most sublime ways of God. Common life is to them a daily revelation, and their attention feeds itself on its events. Thus the Blessed Mother becomes our teacher in the method of listening to and profiting by the daily teachings of our Lord."

2. "And indeed we may well here remind ourselves of the immense dignity and grandeur of the life of ordinary Christians in the Catholic Church. Do we not live among the same mysteries as those in the midst of which that Blessed Mother spent her life after the Annunciation? We are daily conversant with the Presence of our Lord in the Blessed Sacrament; whether in the Holy Mass, which is a repetition of Calvary, or in Holy Communion, or in that perpetual presence in the tabernacle, which is a continuation of the life of Bethlehem and Nazareth. The Precious Blood which was first shed at the Circumcision is continually around us, its application to our souls is made by every sacrament that we receive, and in a thousand other ways. The miracles which encompass our daily life, such as that which is wrought at Holy Mass, are not less miraculous because they are ordinary. It may be said with truth, that if a soul, whose opportunities were not greater than those of an ordinary Christian, could bring itself to catch Our Blessed Lady's thoughtfulness in penetrating the supernatural character of daily incidents, and in tracing in them the workings and ways of God, there would be little more wanting to make that soul the soul of a saint."

3. What, then, were the reflections of Our Lady as she "pondered in her heart" these wonderful events which were happening about her?

## THE CIRCUMCISION

We have her one and only declaration in the Magnificat, which here again she can repeat with emphasized significance. It guides us to the direction of all her thoughts, which is first of all that of the manifestation of God, and of the ways of God, illustrated by this Child that is lying in her arms; the power of God, which so "rules from end to end mightily and disposes all things sweetly"; the liberality of God, Who "so loved the world as to give His only Son"; the faithfulness of God, Who has waited all these years, and now, in "the fulness of time," has "sent His only Son into the world"; the mercy of God, Who has sent His Son that men "may have life, and may have it more abundantly"; and so throughout the whole gamut of the Divine attributes. Then she would see in the Child itself a further and a yet greater illustration of that which she had already recognized in herself. If she was hidden, so was He. If she was patient and obedient, and yet burned with love of God and man, how much more did He?

*Summary*

1. Our Lady the model of the quiet contemplative.
2. The supernatural element in everyday life.
3. The thoughts of Our Lady over the Crib.

## VII.—THE CIRCUMCISION

*"And after eight days were accomplished, that the Child should be circumcised, His name was called*

## THE PRINCE OF PEACE

*Jesus, which was called by the Angel before He was conceived in the womb."—Luke ii. 21.*

1. We recognize at once in the simple narrative of these lives the immediate decision of Our Lady and St. Joseph that they will make no difference between themselves and others because of the Child that has been given to them. Other parents submit their children to the law by a certain definite ceremony; they will do the same with theirs, though they know Him to be above the law. Here as always their rule is that unless they receive some special intimation from above they will do the ordinary thing; probably indeed they were themselves so ordinary, and natural, and like everybody else, that it never occurred to them to act otherwise. We watch this characteristic working throughout the life of the Holy Family; Mary and Joseph act differently from others only when they have a special mandate to do so, and sometimes when that mandate might have been expected it does not come.

2. In this ceremony our Lord performs His first public act as man. He is born a Jew, under the law; therefore, as He said of Himself on a very similar occasion, when submitting to the baptism of John, it "behoved Him to fulfil all justice." On both occasions there is no question of His own individual need; but there is a distinct declaration that He has made common cause with those who did need it. Circumcision

## THE CIRCUMCISION

had been enjoined on Abraham and his children as a sign of the covenant made with Him by God. It was a mark of these children, and of their faith in the promises of God. It implied also, as St. Paul teaches, the obligation to keep the Mosaic Law, once that Law had become established. Our Lord accepted Circumcision, as it were, upon these terms. His Circumcision fulfilled and gave power to all the circumcisions which had been administered under the covenant with Abraham, even as His Sacrifice gave power to all the sacrifices that had gone before. He then took away the rite once for all, in the new Christian Sacrament of Baptism, even as in the Sacrifice of the New Law He closed the sacrifices of the old.

3. Catholic contemplation dwells upon the Circumcision as the first shedding of the Precious Blood. We feel with Mary and St. Joseph, who saw in this blood-shedding the beginning of our Lord's life of bodily suffering. We feel that they must have known, even if only dimly, that this ceremony was of great significance both for the past and for the future; that the blood-shedding of Abel, and of all who had suffered or were to suffer, was in some way to find in this Child its sanction, its antitype, its consummation; that therefore through much blood-shedding would that Child come to His own. And on the other hand there was joy in their hearts at this further realization of the

faithfulness of God. Now at last, with the Precious Blood of Christ, the "Lamb that was slain from the beginning of the world," was the price of man's redemption being paid. The blood of man, drawn from Our Lady's own veins, was now at last of value sufficient to atone, because it became the blood of the Son of God. Upon this thought St. Paul continually meditates.

*Summary*

1. The simplicity of the Holy Family, making itself exactly like others in spite of its honor, is nowhere more manifest than in the story of the Circumcision.

2. The Circumcision itself is the fulfilment of the Covenant in a double sense.

3. This first shedding of the Precious Blood is the beginning of the great work of Atonement, with all its sorrows and all its joy.

## VIII.—THE HOLY NAME OF JESUS

*"His name was called Jesus, which was called by the Angel before He was conceived in the womb."— Luke ii. 21.*

1. It is not difficult to meditate upon the Holy Name, or to use the Holy Name in prayer. More than any other name, perhaps alone among all proper names, it is appropriate to the One Who owned it. Usually the names of men are given at random; they mean nothing in themselves; a man who happens to be called John might just as well have been called Thomas or William; the mere name tells us nothing about

## THE HOLY NAME OF JESUS

him; it is a convenient means of distinguishing him from others, a label put upon him and little or no more. With a few human beings it has been otherwise: Adam, Abraham, Josue, John the Baptist were given names that signified the men on whom they were bestowed. But with none is this so true as it is with our Lord and Savior Jesus Christ. With care the Angel impressed it on His Mother's mind: "Thou shalt call His name Jesus," he said, and there followed the description of His future greatness. With care it was repeated to Joseph: "Thou shalt call His name Jesus, for He shall save His people from their sins."

2. The Name stands as a complete summary and description of our Lord's character and office, and it is under this aspect that it has been regarded by thousands of saints, whose hearts have melted at its mere sound. To them Jesus is their God, Jesus is their King, Jesus is their Redeemer, Jesus is their Mediator, Jesus is the Savior, Jesus is their great Priest, Jesus is their Intercessor, Jesus is the Captain under Whom they fight, Jesus is the Leader Whom they follow, Jesus is their Teacher, Jesus is the Giver of their law, Jesus is the Spouse and Shepherd of their souls, Jesus is their Light, Jesus is their Life, Jesus is the Judge before Whom they rejoice to think that they must one day stand, Jesus is their final and eternal Reward, for which alone they live.

3. But He is also to them the mirror of all the most glorious and winning virtues. He is, and His Name tells them that He is, unbounded Charity, infinite Mercy, extremest Kindness, deepest Humility, most devoted Piety, Chastity without a stain. It is the prerogative of love to transform those who love into the likeness of Him Whom they love; and as the mere name of one who is loved cannot sound in the ear or be thought of in the mind without adding to the love which is already there, so the thought of the Holy Name and the mention of the Holy Name have a kind of sacramental power in the hearts of His saints. They seem to convey the grace which enable men to think like Him, to speak like Him, to act like Him, to sacrifice themselves like Him, and to Him, and for Him, and along with Him, to make Him known to others, not by word only, but also by reproduction of Him in themselves, and to win all men to love Him.

*Summary*

1. Unlike other names, the Holy Name of Jesus both designates Him to whom it is given, and is a summary description of His life and character.
2. Then to the saints it is an ever-sufficient subject of contemplation, spreading its rays of meaning out as from a central sun.
3. And it is an all-sufficient source of inspiration to a perfect life, seeing that Jesus is what He is, and love of Jesus makes us like to Him, and the name of Jesus fosters this love.

## IX.—THE HOLY NAME OF JESUS (continued)

*"Bless the Lord, O my soul, and let all that is within thee bless His holy Name. Bless the Lord, O my soul, and never forget all He hath done for thee."*—Ps. cii. 1, 2.

1. The great saint of the Holy Name is St. Bernardine of Siena. In his missionary expeditions he carried it in a banner, and used it continually in his sermons. He has a long treatise on the Holy Name, which teems with matter for prayer. The Holy Name, he says, is first of all fruitful for beginners. For these, for sinners, "it shows the immense mercifulness of God, it enables a devout man to gain a victory in every conflict, whether with the devil, the flesh, or the world, it has the power of healing sickness when rightly used, it fills with joy and exultation those who are in any adversity." He quotes St. Peter, that "through His name all receive remission of sins who believe in Him"; St. John: "Your sins are forgiven you for His name's sake"; St. Peter again: "There is no other name under heaven given to men whereby we must be saved"; the prayer of the Church in the Acts of the Apostles, that God would "stretch forth his hand to signs and cures and wonders, to be done by the name of thy only Son Jesus"; the further statement in the Acts, that the Apostles went forth "from the presence of the Council, rejoicing that they were ac-

counted worthy to suffer reproach for the name of Jesus."

2. Next it is fruitful for the proficient. "It is cherished in their hearts and fed upon by faith, it is taken into their mouths and preached or spoken about, it is made the spring of their actions, which then become a great accummulation of merits, it is appropriated in a new way by perseverance, and then it becomes a principle of abiding and enduring life, the remedy of the frailty and fickleness which belong to our poor nature." By virtue of this Holy Name, he tells us, we ourselves have become the sons of God. In the virtue of this Holy Name St. Paul placed all his hope of doing good. The power of the Holy Name is the power of the Holy Ghost. And for its power of endurance he asks: "Art thou not refreshed as often as thou rememberest the name of Jesus? What is there equal to it for the feeding of the mind that thinks of it, for repairing weariness, for strengthening virtues, for nourishing good and upright ways, for fostering true affections?"

3. Lastly it is fruitful for those whom he calls the perfect. The first fruit is "the sweetness with which those who meditate upon it are filled," according to the beautiful rhythm of St. Bernard's, *Jesu dulcis memoria*. The second is the wonderful power which this Holy Name gives to the prayers and petitions of the devout soul. The third is the immense sweetness which

## THE PURIFICATION

it gives to those who continually renew its memory. The fourth is the triumph and glory which it will produce in eternity: " 'They shall glory in Thee, all who love Thy name.' And thus for the sake of the name of Jesus the whole soul will live, and be endowed and enriched and beautified with all its powers; it will be made like to God three and one, united to Him, enlightened by Him, and plunged in perfect peace through Him, for it is to live for ever in the state of perfect bliss, furnished with the accumulation of all good."

### Summary

1. The Holy name is the secret of support for sinners and beginners.

2. It is the inspiration for every thought, word, and deed of those more advanced.

3. It is the joy of those who may be thought perfect, their source of contemplation, their power in prayer, the final reward.

## X.—THE PURIFICATION

*"And after the days of her Purification, according to the Law of Moses, were accomplished, they carried Him to Jerusalem, to present Him to the Lord. As it is written in the Law of the Lord, That every male opening the womb shall be called holy to the Lord: and to offer sacrifice, according as it is written in the Law of the Lord, a pair of turtle doves, or two young pigeons."*—Luke ii. 22-24.

1. The story of Christmas, crowded as it is, is quickly told and quickly over. The Holy

Family do not give themselves much time to loiter. First, they fulfil the custom binding on all the children of Abraham, then they fulfil the law binding all the children of Moses. The mother was "unclean" until she had presented herself at the temple and made her offering, and received the absolution of the priest; the first-born, if a boy, was by right the child of the temple, and must be bought back by the parents that it might remain their own. Here, then, we find the Immaculate Mother with the utmost simplicity in the world, without a thought that it should be otherwise, eager only that the Law should be observed, and that the blessing of God should be upon her, counting herself as defiled, and letting others count her as defiled, at a moment which, of all others, was the triumph of a virgin's innocence.

2. The presentation of our Lord rests on another basis. This had become part of the Law as a commemoration of the deliverance from Egypt. In the law we read: "When the Lord shall have brought thee into the land of the Canaanite, as he swore to thee and to thy fathers, and shall give it to thee, thou shalt set apart all that openeth the womb to the Lord, and all that is first brought forth of thy cattle, whatsoever thou shalt have of the male sex, thou shalt consecrate to the Lord. And every first-born of men thou shalt redeem with a price. And when thy son shall ask thee tomorrow,

## THE PURIFICATION

What is this? thou shalt answer him. With a strong hand did the Lord bring us forth out of the land of Egypt, out of the house of bondage; for when Pharaoh was hardened and would not let us go, the Lord slew every first-born in the land of Egypt, from the first-born of man to the first-born of beasts, therefore I sacrifice to the Lord all that openeth the womb of the male sex, and all the first-borns of my sons I redeem.... It shall be a sign in thy hand, and as a thing hung between thine eyes, for a remembrance, because the Lord hath brought us forth out of Egypt with a strong hand." Thus did our Lord link up in Himself the type and its fulfilment; the deliverance which had been, and the greater deliverance at His later and greater self-oblation.

3. And this was the first occasion on which our Lord came into His Father's house. He was to come to it again in many capacities; in a few years as a disciple; once more fulfilling the custom of the law; later as an indignant purifier, when "the zeal of His Father's house would consume Him"; later again as a teacher and worker of miracles; then as a triumphant king on Palm Sunday; and finally, when He would denounce from its steps its priests and its masters, and would leave it never to return. Then the Temple would pass away, not a stone being left upon a stone; and instead our Lord

*THE PRINCE OF PEACE*

would again be presented to His Father in countless temples throughout the world.

*Summary*

1. In the Purification Our Lady reckons herself with the defiled.
2. In the Presentation Our Lord is Himself the completion of the type of the deliverance.
3. The coming to His Temple, then and now.

## XI.—SIMEON

*"And, behold, there was a man in Jerusalem named Simeon, and this man was just and devout, waiting for the consolation of Israel, and the Holy Spirit was in him. And he had received an answer from the Holy Spirit, that he should not see death before he had seen the Christ of the Lord. And he came by the Spirit into the Temple. And when His Parents brought in the Child Jesus, to do for Him according to the custom of the Law, he also took Him into his arms, and blessed God."—Luke ii. 25-28.*

1. Holy Simeon is a figure in the history of the Jews which is full of significance. Just as Zachary and Elizabeth could not have been alone, but must have had many associates, faithful to the true tradition of the Messias like themselves; just as the families from which Mary and Joseph came could not have been the only faithful households, but must have been associated with many others; so Simeon, and later the prophetess Anna, must have been two among many who were faithful in "looking for the consolation of Israel." Of all that faithful background the whole of the New Testament tells us

*SIMEON*

practically nothing; but one may say that in this the Gospels do not differ from history in general. In all times, under all circumstances, underneath the excitements of life which history most loves to record, there has always been, and there still always is, a great ocean of goodness on which the world ultimately relies.

2. Hence Simeon helps us to restore a right perspective in our estimates of mankind. We are always prone to make sweeping condemnations, forgetting that all generalizations of individual men must always be inaccurate. Though Bethlehem had no home for our Lord, not all the people of Bethlehem were His enemies; Bethlehem was the home of the Holy Innocents and their suffering mothers. Though the Jews of Jerusalem rejected Him, yet not all were opposed to Him; we have enough in Simeon and others like him to prove this. And so in our own time no matter who may be our adversaries, temporal or spiritual, we may be sure that in their ranks there are many sincere and single-minded, looking, like ourselves, according to their lights, "for the consolation of Israel." And perhaps especially is this true of the Jews.

3. Simeon was apparently no man of action; he seems to have done nothing in particular. He may or may not have been a priest in the temple; St. Luke does not say so, though some may well argue that his part in this scene would imply it. But he was "just and devout"; he

was true in his life and spiritual in his mind; he was a man of prayer, looking to the great end, and receiving communications from God. He was a contemplative, with a clean heart, and the two qualities gave him all he needed, the power to recognize our Lord when he met Him. "Blessed are the clean of heart, for they shall see God." Such a man is led "by the Spirit"; such a man is tried, but at the end of the trial it is given him to "take the Child into his arms, and to bless God."

*Summary*

1. Simeon reminds us of the multitude of faithful souls who were looking for "the consolation of Israel."
2. He reminds us that there are many such outside our own ranks today.
3. The prayerful nature of Simeon is the nature which most easily recognizes Our Lord.

## XII.—THE CANTICLE OF SIMEON

*"And [he] said: Now thou dost dismiss thy servant, O Lord, according to thy word, in peace; because my eyes have seen thy salvation, which thou hast prepared before thy people: a light to the revelation of the Gentiles, and the glory of thy people Israel. And his father and mother were wondering at these things which were spoken concerning him."*
—Luke ii. 25-28.

1. This, then, is "the consolation of Israel" for which Simeon and his companions had been yearning; and the moment it comes, though it be represented only by a tiny Child lying in his

## THE CANTICLE OF SIMEON

arms it is enough to make life no longer of value, enough to give him peace for all eternity. His Canticle is the last in the great trilogy. Mary had opened it with the Magnificat; Zachary had taken up Our Lady's song and had developed part of it in the Benedictus; Simeon now carries on the thought of Zachary and dwells on the mercies of the Lord to the world. He begins with thanksgiving for the great grace granted to himself; echoing the words of Jacob at the recovery of Joseph: "Now shall I die with joy, because I have seen thy face, and leave thee alive"; and yet more those of the elder Tobias: "Now, O Lord, do with me according to Thy will, and command my spirit to be received in peace." He had been permitted to see, not merely a consolation for himself, but "Thy salvation," the "consolation of Israel."

2. Then he develops this "salvation," and in a way that may well astonish us. Hitherto we have felt the Jews preoccupied with the thought of the Messias as being their special Redeemer; and we have felt all sympathy with their mind. But here on a sudden, from the most intense circle of the Jewish expectation, comes an outburst which proves that the prospect before them reached far beyond the children of Abraham; it extends to and includes the whole world. The Child is to be a light, not for the Jews only but for the enlightenment of all nations; on this account He is to be the glory of God's people,

Israel. This is the aspect of prophecy on which Simeon lays hold, that aspect which the less faithful Jews seem to have neglected, for while the latter clung to the Messias as their King, many prophets had foretold Him "as the desired of all nations," Who "hath revealed His justice in the sight of the Gentiles." In this sense, then, while Zachary looks to the fulfilment of the past, Simeon already opens the new era and looks to fulfilment in the future.

3. The sentence which follows is surely the sentence of Our Lady herself. Who else would have said of her that she "wondered at these things?" Who else would have given Joseph the first place? "And his father and mother were wondering at these things which were spoken concerning him." At what did they wonder? The evidence of the Magnificat alone is enough to show that to Mary there was nothing very new in these words of Simeon; and the prophecy concerning herself had not yet been uttered. Is it not the wonder which every saint, which every contemplative experiences in the ever deeper understanding of the truths of revelation? We know what is meant by Christ our Lord, but from time to time, in Communion, in prayer, in times of suffering, we seem to see, not merely to know. Then we, too, "marvel"; as perhaps did Our Lady at such times as this.

*Summary*

1. Simeon's consolation is enough to make their

## THE PROPHECY OF SIMEON

life and all that it contains, joy or sorrow, few or many days, of no account.

2. His consolation extends not to his own people only, but to all the world.

3. And the parents wondered, marvelled; what was the nature of their marvelling?

## XIII.—THE PROPHECY OF SIMEON

*"And Simeon blessed them, and said to Mary his Mother: Behold this child is set for the ruin and for the resurrection of many in Israel, and for a sign which shall be contradicted; and thy own soul a sword shall pierce, that out of many hearts thoughts may be revealed."—Luke ii. 34-35.*

1. We have already had prophecies concerning the future life of the Child. The Angel has said that "He shall be great"; Zachary has proclaimed His mission; the choir of angels have spoken to the shepherds of His Kingship. But no one has yet recorded that part of His future which is most distinctly marked in Isaias, the lot of suffering. No one has alluded to that discriminating character of His mission which is announced by the prophet Malachy. "Behold He cometh, said the Lord of hosts, and who shall be able to think of the day of His coming, and who shall stand to see Him? For He is like a refining fire, and like the fuller's herb." This last is the first part of Simeon's prophecy: The Child is to be a rock of offence to many, and to many—more, may we not add?—He is to be the resurrection.

2. The second part of the prophecy refers to the Child Himself and His Mother. He Himself is to go through the agony of contradiction; she must suffer along with Him. Already for Our Lady the sympathetic pain of the Passion is beginning; already her "Behold the handmaid of the Lord" is bearing fruit. A fond mother suffers untold secret agony in her heart when she watches her child and wonders about its future; perhaps she would suffer more if she knew all. And Mary, if she did not know all, at least knew enough from this moment to have the sword continually cutting through her heart.

3. Then follows, apparently, the reason for all this: "That out of many hearts thoughts may be revealed." As so often in the Scripture, above all in the prophecies of Scripture, in both the Old Testament and the New, one suddenly comes upon a sentence which seems to contain an infinity of meaning, which we cannot hope to fathom, which it would be mere presumption on our parts to attempt to fathom, and yet which affords us an endless source of contemplation. Put it in a kind of litany, and see how indeed the prophecy has been and is being fulfilled. "This Child is set for the fall of many—that out of many hearts thoughts may be revealed. This Child is set for the resurrection of many —that out of many hearts thoughts may be revealed. This Child is set for a sign that shall be contradicted—that out of many hearts

thoughts may be revealed. Thy own soul a sword shall pierce—that out of many hearts thoughts may be revealed." In such a way it is not difficult for my own thoughts to be discovered.

### Summary

1. The Child is to be for the fall of many, and for the resurrection of many.
2. The Child and His Mother are to suffer in the task.
3. The motive: "that out of many hearts thoughts may be revealed."

## XIV.—THE WITNESS OF ANNA

*"And there was a prophetess called Anna, the daughter of Phanuel, of the tribe of Aser: she was far advanced in years, and had lived with her husband seven years from her virginity. And she was a widow until four score and four years, who departed not from the Temple, by fastings and prayers serving day and night. Now she, at the same hour, coming in, gave praise to the Lord, and spoke of him to all that looked for the redemption of Israel. And after they had performed all things according to the law of the Lord, they returned into Galilee, to their own city Nazareth."—Luke ii. 36-39.*

1. "As some of the Fathers of the Church tell us, no class, age, or sex was to be left out in the homage which was to be paid to our Lord in His infancy." Poor and rich were to be there, innocent children and the aged, men and women, those in the world and those consecrated to the service of God; and among these it is peculiarly

## THE PRINCE OF PEACE

fitting that a place should be found for a representative of that class which seems to grow with the growth of time and which is of incalculable service to God's cause. I speak of the devoted women workers who have been conspicuous in the Church from the beginning; who followed our Lord and His apostles and ministered to them, who were specially dear to St. Paul and were constantly mentioned by Him, who shine conspicuously in the ages of martyrdom, being the protectors of the bones of martyrs and often the saviors of popes and confessors, who throughout history have been the occasion of the spread of the faith, and who today, by their lives, by their influence, by their prayer, by their active cooperation, are in a true sense the support of the Church.

2. A patron of this class of women is Anna; not, apparently, bound by any vow, but a widow, living in the world, devoting herself to prayer, and mortification, and the service of the altar. To such souls it is given to see more than others; in some mysterious way their knowledge of the supernatural grows from more to more; they have an instinct for the truth, and many a theologian has learned from a word of theirs something which his study has never reached. Such souls, too, have a power in their words; without knowing it themselves their constant union with and service of God enables them to "give praise to the Lord, and to speak of

## THE WITNESS OF ANNA

Him to all that look for the redemption of Israel." We need not then look far for the source of Anna's discovery of the Child in Simeon's arms.

3. All the first act has now been played. The manifestation had been made to all classes, and the Holy Family could retire with their treasure from the stage. St. Luke tells us that "after they had performed all things according to the law of the Lord they returned into Galilee, to their city Nazareth." This raises the difficulty about the story of the Wise Men at Bethlehem, told by St. Matthew. But the difficulty should not be great. St. Luke for some reason has not chosen to tell the story over again; hence he links up his narration of the Nativity with that which is to follow, in a comprehensive sentence such as is not uncommon in the Gospels. The retiring nature of the family is what he has most in mind, and he lets that alone appear.

### Summary

1. Anna the prophetess represents the women workers in the Church, who have always been a great source of blessing.
2. She represents their work and she witnesses to their reward.
3. The family went back into retirement.

## XV.—THE STAR IN THE EAST

*"Now when Jesus was born in Bethlehem of Juda, in the days of King Herod, behold, there came Wise Men from the East to Jerusalem, saying, Where is he that is born King of the Jews? for we have seen His star in the East, and we are come to adore Him."*—Matt. ii. 1, 2.

1. We are here in touch with one of those mysterious events in the life of our Lord which baffle all human comprehension. We set aside the miracles and other supernatural interferences such as the apparitions of angels, which are "natural" enough in the wider sense; apart from these are one or two scenes before which human criticism is wholly baffled. This visit of the Magi is one; the Transfiguration is another; the falling down of the mob before our Lord in the Garden is a third; the culmination of them all is found in the Resurrection. For miracles and other like events rationalism has found self-satisfying explanation; for these it has no explanation, it can only say that they did not happen. Even Catholic science adds little to our knowledge. It can only guess; and if at times an astronomer works out a theory about the star, or a geographer tells us whence the Magi came, we can only add that possibly there may be something in what they say, but that every theory hitherto adduced bristles with difficulties and objections.

## THE STAR IN THE EAST

2. Who were these Wise Men? We do not know. Whence did they come? We do not know. How had they their knowledge? We do not know. What led them to Jerusalem instead of, say, to Alexandria, or Athens, or Rome, or even to their own capital, wherever that may have been? We do not know. All we do know is that out of the darkness of the surrounding paganism there suddenly emerged, not some stray numbers of the Chosen People, not some of those wanderers who still abode weeping by the waters of Babylon, but utter strangers, aliens in blood and creed, to whom everything Jewish was unknown, who, from their language at least, might be supposed to be astrologers, worshippers of a kind that were classed in the utter condemnation of idolatry. "We have seen His star, we pagans, we sages, we outcasts, we despised Asiatic Gentiles. And we have come to adore in what way we know how; not in your temple, not according to your Mosaic rite, but in what way we know how, as pagans can." What a lesson and a warning is here!

3. The story finds its anticipation in another story in the Old Testament, and the one may very well be the key to the other. The Jews were making their way to the Promised Land. A pagan prophet, a heathen, was called upon to curse them. He came, but in spite of himself his words could only frame a blessing; and his blessing was one of the most detailed proph-

ecies that the Old Testament contains. "I shall see him," he cried, "but not now. I shall behold him, not near. A star shall rise out of Jacob, and a sceptre shall spring up from Israel, and shall strike the chiefs of Moab, and shall waste all the children of Seth." One grand thought at least rises out of this mystery. Though the Jews were indeed the Chosen People, yet all mankind was God's people none the less. Though the Jews had "Moses and the prophets," yet all men had also the guiding hand of God upon them. Though the Jews lived in the sunlight of God's favor, yet even in the darkness around there were still God's moon and stars. And, thank God, the same is true today. Even in the darkness God is there.

*Summary*

1. We cannot hope to fathom this mystery of the Magi and their coming.
2. They prove to us that God's guiding hand was not taken from the pagan world.
3. They fulfil the prophecy of Balaam.

## XVI.—THE MAGI IN JERUSALEM

*"And Herod the King hearing this, was troubled, and all Jerusalem with him. And assembling together all the chief priests and the scribes of the people, he inquired of them where Christ should be born. But they said to him, In Bethlehem of Juda: for as it is written by the Prophet: And thou, Beth-*

## THE MAGI IN JERUSALEM

*lehem, the land of Juda, art not the least among the princes of Juda: for out of thee shall come forth the ruler, who shall rule my people Israel. Then Herod, privately calling the Wise Men, inquired of them diligently the time of the star's appearing to them. And sending them into Bethlehem, said, Go, and search diligently after the Child, and when you have found Him, bring me word again, that I also may come and adore Him."*—Matt. ii. 3-8.

1. It is proverbial, it is illustrated again and again in history and in literature, that the greatest unbelievers, above all those who are faithless with a bad conscience, are the most superstitious people in the world. Herod is no exception to this rule; one may say his character is fairly well analyzed in Shakespeare's Macbeth, except that the latter had at least an early record that was clean. He was dominated by superstitious fears, buoyed up by superstitious hopes; the coming of the Magi was one more of the influences that guided him in the merciless plans he was for ever framing. But "the chief priests and scribes"—what are we to think of them? What a contrast is this recognition of prophecy to that last cry before another ruler: "We have no King but Cæsar." Here at least they accepted the evidence; they were not interested enough to question or deny it; its significance, and therefore their opposition, would develop later.

2. But there is perhaps no passage in the New Testament which more clearly displays the

mind of the Jews than this. It is agreed by all, Christians and non-Christians alike, that they were full of the spirit of prophecy. Not only did they accept direct prophecy as they had received it, but they took the whole record of the Old Testament as prophetic; they interpreted passage after passage in a prophetic sense, though literally they had not such meaning, even the events and persons in their past history they held to be significant of the Christ that was to come, And the Holy Spirit guided them in their interpretation; as this, and several other passages quoted by the evangelists show, they were not wrong, even though they proved themselves utterly unworthy of the guidance. Though men fail Him, God still keeps His Church infallible.

3. The Magi came into Jerusalem, and found the "faithful" Jews seemingly indifferent. They made their inquiries in all simplicity, and found they had created a hubbub. The Church of Jerusalem had apparently gone to sleep, and was so roused to a fever by these strangers knocking at the door. Light and grace had come from an unexpected quarter, in an unexpected moment, and the "faithful" did not know what to make of it. Clearly it was light, clearly it was grace; but light and grace are sometimes annoying to those who have settled down in a contentment of indifference. They would send these Wise Men on; they themselves would not

## THE ADORATION OF THE MAGI

move. If the King should afterwards be found to suit their turn, they could take up His cause later; if not, they could remain where they were. There was another alternative; but that at the time did not trouble them. It was continued in the King's own words: "He that is not with Me is against Me."

### Summary

1. The character of Herod and of the chief priests and scribes.
2. The Jewish mind in regard to prophecy.
3. The treatment of the Magi in Jerusalem.

## XVII.—THE ADORATION OF THE MAGI

*"And when they had heard the King they went their way, and behold, the star which they had seen in the East went before them, until it came and stood over where the Child was. And seeing the star they rejoiced with great joy. And going into the house they found the Child and Mary his Mother, and falling down they adored him; and opening their treasures they offered to him gifts, gold, frankincense and myrrh."—Matt. ii. 9-11.*

1. There is an astonishing simplicity about these Wise Men from the East. They trust the blind guidance of a star; they entrust themselves to an unknown people in Jerusalem; they trust a King whose reputation for treachery is notorious; they go again on their way full of trust; and they are rewarded first by the guidance of the star, and then by the fulfilment of

*THE PRINCE OF PEACE*

all their best hopes. It is the way of God; there are some virtues in whose exercise He seems to take special delight; and to secure this He will play with His children. Among them conspicuous are faith, and hope, and charity. He will make things appear impossible that they may assert their faith the more; He will darken the way that they may the more emphasize their hope; He will take Himself away, that they may appeal the more vehemently in love. But "He is faithful"; and to such as He tries He gives the power to respond, and to such as respond He gives the guiding star and Himself.

2. "Seeing the star they rejoiced with great joy." The words obviously imply that the days in Jerusalem had been painful days, days of darkness and trial, perhaps even of ridicule and insult. The King, it is true had treated them with a show of interest; but the attitude of the rest, from the mere fact that none cared to go with them to act even as a guide, seems to show come contempt and opposition. But now their joy returned, and soon it was complete. "And entering into the house"—thank God, we say, it was now a house, and no longer the cold cave—"they found the young Child, with Mary his Mother." It is remarkable that St. Matthew should so emphasize the Mother, and should even add her name, Mary. Would not "they found the Child" have been enough? Would not "they found the Child and His Mother" have been

## THE ADORATION OF THE MAGI

enough? This little word alone shows us that St. Matthew was no less devoted to that Mother than was St. Luke or St. John.

3. The Gentile Church has always dwelt upon the scene which follows. So deeply did it in the early days associate itself with this act of adoration that the feast of the Epiphany was held with greater pomp than the feast of Christman; even until now its octave is in one sense of greater rank, and there are parts of England where it is still called "Old Christmas Day." "They adored Him," acknowledging Him as the King Whom they sought. Did they know Him to be also God? They offered Him the best that they had; the tiny offering signified their desire to give Him all; nothing in their eyes was too good, nothing should be kept back. This is enough; when we speak of such worshippers believing our Lord to be God we know not what we say. He was the One; He was the Master of the stars; He was worthy of all worship; what need we more?

### Summary

1. The simple confidence of the Magi met with its reward of consolation.
2. The consolation was found, first in the guidance from Heaven, then in the finding of "the Child, with Mary, his Mother."
3. Their adoration begins the unending adoration of the nations.

## XVIII.—THE RETURN OF THE MAGI

*"And having received an answer in sleep that they should not return to Herod, they went back another way into their own country."—Matt. ii. 12.*

1. The Magi stayed with our Lord and His Mother; as St. John says of the first disciples who met Him, "They came, and saw, and abode with Him all that day." It would be well for us if we could fathom something of the revelation that was then given to them, something of the meaning in their words when, with the disciples they could say: "We have found the Lord." They "saw His glory" and His power; had He not commanded the stars, and made them act as guides to these His worshippers? Had He not commanded their own hearts, and guided them aright in their reaching of these wonders? They saw His faithfulness. Whatever origin is to be given to this knowledge of the Magi, it must at least be said that they were inheritors of a long tradition. They had not the accumulated possession of the Jews; but long before the Jews were chosen and set apart from the rest of mankind the promise had begun to be made. Adam was not a Jew; Noe was not a Jew; Melchisedech was not a Jew; Abraham, and Isaac, and Jacob, and Joseph, and Moses had faithful kinsfolk who were not Jews; and it would have been strange if among all their descendants the record of the promise had per-

## THE RETURN OF THE MAGI

ished. God had been faithful, not to the Jews only, but to all the world besides.

2. If thoughts such as these must have reigned in the hearts of the Magi, no less deep must have been the thoughts of Mary as she watched these strangers falling down and adoring. "Behold from henceforth all generations shall call me blessed." Already her prophecy was being fulfilled. "A light for the revelation of the nations"; already the words of Simeon were coming true. Again God had shown His illuminating power; first to the shepherds on the hill, then to Simeon and Anna, and now to these strangers in a foreign land. And like them, these men had obeyed. Though their light had been less they had followed; though the labor to be undertaken had been greater they had undertaken it; though the prospect of reward was all but nothing they had not hesitated. "Amen, I say to you; I have not found so great faith in Israel," said our Lord later of a pagan centurion; and we can fancy Our Lady saying the same as she looked down upon and blessed these Gentile Magi.

3. The end of their visit came and they must tear themselves away. Whither did they go? We do not know. What became of them? We do not know. We have a tradition, but only a tradition; we really know nothing. Out of the darkness they came, into the darkness they returned; no more Jews than before, though

they possessed in their hearts the treasure of treasures. And if Anna went away and "spoke of Him to all that looked for the redemption of Israel"; if of the shepherds it is said that "all they that heard wondered, and at those things that were told them"; then we may be sure that the same may be said of the Magi. They were the first apostles. Somewhere outside the Holy Land Christ had been made known, somewhere the good tidings was spread, though the world knows nothing of it now. But how little do we know of the working of the Holy Spirit, above all outside the Church!

*Summary*

1. The thoughts of the adoring Magi.
2. The thoughts of Our Lady, pondering in her heart.
3. The Magi returned to their own country.

## XIX.—PERSECUTION

*"And when they were departed, behold, an Angel of the Lord appeared in sleep to Joseph, saying, Arise and take the Child and His Mother, and fly into Egypt, and be there until I shall tell thee. For it will come to pass that Herod will seek the Child to destroy Him.—Matt. ii. 13.*

1. Our Lady has already learned that the hand of God invariably bestows its favors in two parts; if there is intense joy as one ingredient, the other is also intense suffering. The Nativity was a scene of joy, but it was also a scene of utter poverty and seemingly of needless privation. The conferring of the Holy Name of Jesus

## PERSECUTION

was a glad ceremony, but it was accompanied with the first blood-shedding of her little Child. The joy of the Presentation, and of her own Purification, had been followed immediately by the promise of the sword of sorrow. Hence, when she looked upon the Magi pouring out their treasures and their hearts at the feet of her Son, saying, "I have found Him Whom my soul loveth, I have held Him and will not let Him go," she might well have asked herself what new trial was in store for them, for her Child, for Joseph, and for herself.

2. And we may well carry her reflection further, for there is scarcely any scene in the life of our Lord which is more prophetic than this scene of the flight into Egypt. "By the sweat of thy brow shalt thou eat bread." So had God spoken to Adam, and through Adam to the whole human race. Out of love for man He decreed that suffering should be his lot; and in one sense the more He loved the more He would permit man to suffer. He should suffer by failure, he should suffer in himself, he should suffer most of all from his fellowmen, by persecution. God would not interfere when man rose unjustly against man. When malice more than human—for such has invariably been the mark of persecution—rose against His own, He would not put out His hand to prevent it. Those He loved, His Church, His saints, His individual followers in the secrets of the hearts, should

## THE PRINCE OF PEACE

have the fullest share of His favors; but if they were to have most joy in life, they were also to have most sorrow.

3. We need not hope to fathom the complete understanding of all this: that is reserved for the day when "all things have been made new," when the lights and shades in the picture are seen in their perfect setting, when "God shall wipe away all tears from their eyes, and death shall be no more, nor mourning, nor crying, nor sorrow shall be any more, for the former things are passed away." It is enough for us to know that our Lord Himself has specially blessed the persecuted: "Blessed are they that suffer persecution for justice' sake, for theirs is the Kingdom of Heaven." It is enough to know that those who understood Him best "rejoiced that they were accounted worthy to suffer something for the name of Christ." It is enough to see with our own eyes the discipline of persecution, its chastening effect, its power of drawing the best out of humankind, the heroism, the truth of life, the strength of purpose to which it witnesses, and, finally, the honor and glory it wins from God and man alike.

### Summary

1. Suffering as well as joy is the gift of God to those whom He loves best.
2. The same is seen not only in the life of Our Lord but in the life of the whole Church.
3. The reasons are manifold, though we cannot hope to understand them all.

# THE FLIGHT INTO EGYPT

## XX.—THE FLIGHT INTO EGYPT

*"Who, rising up, took the Child and His Mother by night, and retired into Egypt, and he was there until the death of Herod: that it might be fulfilled which the Lord spoke by the prophet saying, Out of Egypt have I called my Son."—Matt. ii. 14, 15.*

1. The reflections on, and the lessons to be drawn from, the flight of the Holy Family into Egypt are obvious and trite, and have been repeated generation after generation. The story is always told to us as illustrating the perfect obedience of the three; of the Child to its early guardians, though Itself so very far above them; of Mary to Joseph, for the time being her superior; of Joseph himself to the obvious will of God, though worldly prudence, justice, wisdom, everything seemed to proclaim against it. And indeed it is a model which has stirred many a follower of Christ to its emulation; when an order has been sudden, when it has been seemingly needless, when it has been subversive of all that has gone before, and yet it has clearly been the place of duty to obey, how often has the example of Joseph and his two dependents enabled and ennobled the soul even of a saint to do its part!

2. This alone might suffice for us here; for there are few thoughts which need to be more pondered by us all. Still it is also well to watch the wonderful hand of God, here as elsewhere, as it were, drawing together the threads of the

*THE PRINCE OF PEACE*

world's history, fulfilling type and prophecy by the hands of those who would gladly have frustrated both, sending His Son into exile in Egypt, because Israel had dwelt there before Him, and because the prophet Osee had said, and had been interpreted to mean, that so it would be done. When the history of mankind is seen in its completeness, how strangely and beautifully will it be found to be linked up in repetitions like this, pattern repeating pattern on the floor of this world, with ever increasing detail, with ever greater glory given to God. The hand of God is never lifted from the guiding rein. Man thinks he does his own will, and in his own limited sphere he is right; but there is a sphere greater than his own, and a will that is also done, with which the will of man cannot compare.

3. And next there is the fact that God's ways are so different from ours. He might have given the Holy Family a longer warning than that of a few minutes; but He did not. He might have hidden them in some more convenient place than Egypt—perhaps even Nazareth would have sufficed—but He did not. He might have relieved their anxiety, consulted their condition, helped their necessity in a thousand ways; but He did not. Even in the first instance He might have so arranged that Herod should have known nothing, or that the Magi should have found our Lord in some safer place; but He did not. He has preferred that His own should not be

# *THE HOLY INNOCENTS*

the most comfortable, the most prosperous, the most considered people in this world; to these He has said, and is for ever saying: "Rejoice and be glad, for your reward is exceeding great in heaven."

### Summary

1. The model of obedience in this story is easily understood.
2. The story also shows us the perfect control of the hand of God.
3. Yet that hand directs the world in ways very different from the ways of men.

## XXI.—THE HOLY INNOCENTS

*"Then Herod, perceiving that he was deluded by the Wise Men, was exceedingly angry, and sending, killed all the men-children that were in Bethlehem, and in all the confines thereof, from two years old and under, according to the time which he had diligently inquired of the Wise Men. Then was fulfilled that which was spoken by Jeremies the Prophet, saying: A voice in Rama was heard, lamentation and great mourning, Rachel bewailing her children, and would not be comforted, because they are not."*
—Matt. ii. 16-18.

1. One is appalled at the monstrosity of Herod, a man so steeped in blood that bloodshedding had become his one solution for every difficulty. And yet we know that this is no extraordinary thing. History and the best drama shows us that human nature, corrupted in any one direction, assumes that corruption as part of itself, so that the most unnatural vice becomes

most natural. It is true with every vice, from calumny, and theft, and adultery, to murder, and insubordination, and contempt of God. This is the punishment of vice in this life; the fixing of this state for all eternity is hell. And let it be noticed that every vice, not only that of murder, isolates a man more and more from his fellow-men, makes him their permanent enemy and them his, destroys in him all those qualities which belong to manhood, and leaves him no more than a wild beast, with the added claws and teeth that human intelligence provides.

2. On the other side are Herod's innocent victims. There is much to realize in the fact that they were not willing victims. They were too young to think or to choose; they were passive in their mother's arms and beneath the swords of their executioners; yet the Church has put them in the vanguard of her martyrs. So has it been time and again in the history of the Church; in our own day, when Herod seems to have arisen in so many places, in Asia Minor, in Spain, in Portugal, in Mexico, in Belgium, it would seem to be reaching its climax. In all these places, where victims have been immolated out of hatred for the faith, without any power to say yes or no on their own part, there is for them and for us the joy of knowing that they are now "without spot before the throne of God," witnesses to Him, not only here, but for all eternity. God "chooses whom He

## THE HOLY INNOCENTS

will"; and if those He chooses for death on the battlefield are by us put upon the "Roll of Honor," no less should those be honored whom He chooses for death in His own cause.

3. Thus is the malice of evil-doers everlastingly frustrated. They hack their way through to their own ends, while every victim that they slay not only cries to heaven for vengeance, but also adds to the glory and strength of that which they would fain destroy. Blood that is shed in whatever cause is usually a fruitful seed! and the more noble, the more pure the blood, the better in the distant future is likely to be the harvest. So the nations pride themselves in giving of their best: so God seems to choose the choicest of His children for this honor—witness Fisher, and More, and Campion, and Arundel in our own country—that afterwards, in the fulness of time, "thoughts may be revealed." Rachel may bewail her children, because they are not; but Rachel is the mother of children more numerous than the sands of the seashore.

### Summary

1. Herod, the typical fruit of vice.
2. The Innocents, the vanguard of the martyrs.
3. The fruit of the martyrs is seen in this world and in the next.

## XXII.—THE RETURN FROM EGYPT

*"Now Herod being dead, behold, an Angel of the Lord appeared in sleep to Joseph in Egypt, saying: Rise and take the Child and His Mother, and go into the land of Israel, for they are dead who sought the life of the Child. Who, rising up, took the Child and His Mother, and came into the land of Israel. But hearing that Archelaus reigned in Judaea in the room of Herod his father, he was afraid to go thither, and being warned in sleep, he retired into the parts of Galilee."*—Matt. ii. 19-22.

1. "Herod being dead!" It is no affair of ours to recall the career of this combination of worldly success and human misery, nor the facts of his utterly miserable end. There are few characters in history who might be taken as more typically personifying the character of Satan on earth; the evil fire within his very body, the hatred with which he is rewarded. This man is dead! The Angel does not mention his name; he does not even speak of him as an individual. "They are dead," he says, "who sought the life of the child," as if to draw all thought away from the man himself. He is dead, and at once the work of God revives. It can be checked, it cannot be stopped. There is always some seed left, and when the hindrance is removed it revives. Is there any greater proof of God's work in the world than this its wonderful vitality?

2. The Holy Family "came into the land of Israel." But here again is one of those strange

## THE RETURN FROM EGYPT

dealings of God with man. He had found it good to send an angel to order the return, and that to Israel; but would it not have been just as easy to say, "Go into Nazareth," or "Go into Bethlehem," as "Go into the land of Israel"? Why act so vaguely? Why leave to Joseph the solution of a needless doubt? The order had been given to go into Egypt, and thus a prophecy had been fulfilled; was there not another prophecy which said that "He should be called a Nazarene"? Yes; one may ask question after question, give reason after reason; we do but show that God's ways are not our ways, but that for all that "He ruleth from end to end mightily, and disposeth all things sweetly," both when He guides us clearly and when He bids us walk in the dark, leaving us apparently to our own devices.

3. Joseph obeyed, but evidently not without fear and trembling. His first intention was to settle at Bethlehem, as St. Matthew tells us; but prudence born of fear made him hesitate. He must choose for himself; he must bring his natural powers into play; it must have grown upon him by this time that the Child whose career he was to guide through life was to be marked but little by supernatural signs. Tradition has been so shocked at this that it has attempted to fill up the picture with miraculous events; but Scripture tells us nothing of them, and Joseph is left to his life of perfect faith

and fidelity. So at least he is felt to be left, in almost every step of his career; but at the last he is guided to do the perfect will of God. It was so before the birth of Jesus; it is so now; it is so in the lives of all who have but the will of God before their eyes. Through the gloom that will always guides.

## Summary

1. The work of God revives when the human hindrance is removed.
2. God guides step by step; He will have us often walk in darkness.
3. But He secures that the goal is reached.

## XXIII.—THE CHOICE OF NAZARETH

*"And He came and dwelt in a city called Nazareth, that it might be fulfilled what was said by the Prophet, that He shall be called a Nazarene."—Matt. ii. 23.*

1. St. Matthew has chosen almost all his incidents of the Nativity to show the fulfilment of prophecy. We know from St. Luke that the Annunciation took place at Nazareth; but after that the house must have been given up, and Bethlehem, being the city of David, must have seemed to her and to St. Joseph the most fitting place in which the Son of David should be brought up. But other human reasons drove them from Bethlehem, and the Angel's warning

## THE CHOICE OF NAZARETH

confirmed the conclusion; there was then little choice but to go back to their old abode, and let God work out the rest. Thus another prophecy was to be fulfilled: our Lord was to be born at Bethlehem, but He was to be called a Nazarene. On the cross, long after, our Lord was not to be called: "Jesus of Bethlehem, King of the Jews," for that would have had something of honor and of title about it; but "Jesus of Nazareth, King of the Jews," was altogether too absurd and contradictory. Thus does God play with the prejudices of men.

2. It is well to notice how these men had deluded themselves in this matter. They had interpreted many prophecies aright. They had identified the Messias in many points. They had known He would be born in Bethlehem. But on their own confession they had failed here. "Search the Scriptures," we find them saying later, "and see that out of Galilee a prophet riseth not." And again, on another occasion they asked: "Can any good come out of Nazareth?" Yet St. Matthew gives us the prophecy which they could have known as well as he, which was as explicit as any other, that "He shall be called a Nazarene." How was it that these keen students of Scripture, above all, these searchers into prophecy, failed to discover this one? We may answer this as we would answer another: How was it that they failed, in spite of all their study, to recognize our Lord at all? How is it that,

throughout all time, so many recognize so much of truth as serves their purpose, but the whole truth they will not, and therefore do not see?

3. At the same time it is to be said in their defense that this prophecy quoted by St. Matthew is not clear. As some Fathers say, we should search in vain to find his words in any prophet's work. But probably what is meant is that the word "Nazarene" should be taken in its common sense at that time, which was a sense of contempt—as though He were called a Bœotian, just as in our time we might call a man a Hottentot, or as in America one might be called a "nigger." So St. Matthew sums up in the word "Nazarene" those many prophecies which had described our Lord as "despised, rejected, the outcast of the people"; just those which the Scribes and Pharisees had not found to their liking and had therefore eliminated from their concept of Jesus Christ our Lord.

## Summary

1. "Jesus of Nazareth," a title, "to the Jews a stumbling block and to the Gentiles folly, but to them that believe Christ the power of God and the glory of God."

2. "Jesus of Nazareth," a title which the Jews did not relish, and therefore a title which they failed to recognize.

3. "Jesus of Nazareth," a title beloved by Our Lord Himself, because it made Him "the despised, the rejected."

# THE HIDDEN LIFE

## XXIV.—THE HIDDEN LIFE

*"And the Child grew, and waxed strong, full of wisdom, and the grace of God was in Him."—Luke ii. 40.*

1. A child's life has seldom much to record. When a great man dies, and his biography is written, the first twenty years or more—sometimes it will extend to thirty and even forty years—is usually contained in a single chapter. That chapter will, more often than not, contain a few dates, a few utterly unimportant facts, with one or two traits of budding character more or less significant, and often enough somewhat forced in their interpretation. But this seems to be common among many of the greatest; the greater they have ultimately proved themselves, the more insignificant has their early life been. Witness such names as Cæsar, Napoleon, Wellington, Dante, Shakespeare, Goethe, Aquinas, Suarez, Bourdaloue, St. Gregory the Great, St. Bernard, St. Ignatius Loyola, St. Philip Neri, and almost all the saints who have also proved themselves great in the world's eyes. It is not, then, wonderful that the life of the Greatest of all should have been so hidden, so apparently insignificant.

2. Yet this very insignificance and hiddenness is the light He casts upon humanity at this time. He was "the light of the world," and from the moment of the Nativity that light

never failed. "My father worketh until now," He said on one occasion, "and I also work"; and He never ceased to do the work which had been given to Him from the beginning. In the ages to come the Church was continually to grow among the obscure, and the contemned, and the poor; in the West and the East today we know where we must mainly look for the life and strength of Christianity, indeed the life and strength of all Christian peoples. It is not among the richest; it is not among the mendicants and the poorest; it is among the healthy working classes whose hands are always full, who have more of the real contentment of life than have others, whose contentment leads to a certain generosity of nature, the best ground for the seed of all virtues, whether natural or supernatural. With these, then, does our Lord associate in His days of growth; among these He "waxed strong, full of wisdom."

3. Thus this hidden life is a life of many consecrations. It is the consecration of honorable poverty; it is the consecration of honorable work. It is the consecration of the home and of family life, of the relations between husband and wife, and between parents and children; it is the consecration of that society which is founded upon the family as the unit. It is the consecration of religious life, of the life of seclusion, the life of prayer, the life of poverty, the life of work, all of which religious life in-

cludes, and sanctifies, and teaches by example. It is the consecration, lastly, of that period of life which is so precious, so interesting, so momentous, the time of childhood and adolescence. Our Lord's love of children is well known; His love of those who will help children is well known; when He blessed them, when He protected them, when He set them up as models, when He said, "As often as you do it to the least of these you do it to me," He casts many sidelights on His own early life, His needs, His helps, and the gratitude with which that help was requited.

### Summary

1. The Hidden Life is the life that makes for greatness, material and spiritual.
2. But not on that account is it insignificant or wasted.
3. The Hidden Life of Our Lord has consecrated many elements of modern civilization.

## XXV.—THE LOSS IN THE TEMPLE

*"And His parents went every year to Jerusalem, at the solemn day of the Pasch. And when He was twelve years old they went up to Jerusalem, according to the custom of the feast. And after they had fulfilled the days, when they returned, the Child Jesus remained in Jerusalem, and His parents knew it not. And thinking that He was in the company, they came a day's journey, and sought Him among their kinsfolks and acquaintance. And not finding Him, they returned into Jerusalem, seeking Him."*
—*Luke ii. 41-45.*

1. Of all the scenes in the life of our Lord

one may say there is none more deliberately chosen, more obviously set for an example to many, than this; none which may be more easily understood as a kind of living parable; and yet none which rings with a clearer sense of truth and actuality, on the evidence of the chief sufferer in the scene, Our Blessed Lady. This is the one and only event in the whole life at Nazareth which she has chosen to leave on record; we need to remember this when we look for its interpretation. For there is a sense in which it tells against Our Lady's own authority and place as Mother; therefore she adds her sanction to the limitations of a parent's rights. A child is not a parent's slave; authority does not mean despotism; the essence of good training is that, one day, the child should be his own master, with the power to choose and act for himself.

2. Therefore it was necessary that in this, too, our Lord should be one with His children, whom He loved so much, and defend them from the gentlest, the most subtle, but perhaps the most dangerous of tyrannies. As the age of twelve, so it was understood among the Jews, a boy was master of himself, capable of choosing his path in life, his vocation. For that eventful day his earlier education had prepared him; in the synagogue and school, in the workship, but most at home and at his mother's knee, the child was prepared for the day, when he must

## THE LOSS IN THE TEMPLE

make his own decision. So was it, we are safe in conjecturing, with the Child Who, according to His Mother's account, "waxed strong, full of wisdom, and the grace of God was in Him"; loving words, of a Mother full of love, for a Child that had grown up at her side, and had shown her a Child's true love and duty.

3. But when the time for the great decision came, how violent did it seem! No warning was given; it was made, not in the Mother's quiet home but in His Father's House; the circumstances were such as to aggravate the Mother's agony. The feast was over; they were returning home; after a day's journey the Child was missed; what had become of Him? Had He been already discovered? Had those from whom they had fled to Egypt found Him and killed Him? Had they been wrong in bringing Him to Jerusalem where enemies were known to be living? Or had He chosen some new guardian? What had she done, or not done, to be so left alone? We can easily imagine this sword of sorrow that pierced her heart as she ran back to Jerusalem, as she wandered aimlessly next day seeking for Him Whom her soul loved, willing only what He willed, but craving still to be, if it might be, the "Handmaid of the Lord." The day of separation had come; she had always known it would come; but how differently it had come from what she had expected! How often is it so!

## Summary

1. The story is an obvious declaration of the rights of children, the Christian child's Magna Charta.
2. For this act of choice of vocation His early training had prepared Him.
3. And for the sake of so many parents in after time His Mother's heart was made to suffer.

## XXVI.—THE FINDING IN THE TEMPLE

*"And it came to pass that after three days they found Him in the Temple, sitting in the midst of the doctors, hearing them, and asking them questions. And all that heard Him were astonished at His wisdom and His answers. And seeing Him they wondered. And His Mother said to Him, Son, why hast Thou done so to us? Behold, Thy father and I have sought Thee sorrowing. And He said to them: How is it that you sought Me? did you not know that I must be about My Father's business? And they understood not the word that He spoke unto them."—Luke ii. 46-50.*

1. We have elsewhere seen how our Lord sanctioned and sanctified many phases of human life by His own hidden life at Nazareth. But here we have one special feature as it were taken apart and solemnly consecrated apart; the feature of education. Of course, later in life He sanctified it in abundance by His public life of teaching; but there is a special appropriateness in this earlier consecration, when He Himself was in the rôle of a pupil, and when in this formal way, in the Temple itself, He could solemnly sanctify that all-important work which

## THE FINDING IN THE TEMPLE

the Church has ever claimed for her own. Is it not true to say that there is on earth no more sure means of securing one's own salvation than that of religious teaching, nor any surer way of doing good to others? There is joy for many in this certainty; for many who of all people in the world are perhaps most in need of encouragement.

2. Mary and Joseph found Him in these surroundings. They saw the Child sitting among the listeners; they noticed the attention He had attracted; they read in the faces of the doctors that He had impressed them. How, we do not know; but when Mary "pondered in her heart" all she saw and heard, she must have rejoiced at this first shining of the Light that had come into the world. There was joy in the mere finding of the Child; there was an added joy in finding Him where He was, doing what He was; it was a sign to her of the special work which was near to His heart, and therefore which was near to her own. As we contemplate the scene it seems impossible to believe that her words recorded by St. Luke followed immediately upon the finding of the Child. There was much between; above all the joy. "I have found Him Whom my soul loveth; I have held Him and will not let Him go."

3. But when the first thrill was passed, when she had become sure that He was again her own, then the reflection on the mysterious be-

havior was natural. "They understood not"; even after her Son had spoken they did not understand. So naturally she asked, not complaining, or doubting, as she did not complain or doubt when she asked for understanding at the Annunciation. But the fact was there. For once the Child had given the father and Mother pain, a strange thing indeed. Why? "My Father's business"; no more. Still she "understood not"; how should she? But now she understands. She knows now why on that occasion a sword pierced her soul, "that out of many hearts, thoughts might be revealed." She hears now how for those three days of suffering "all generations have called her blessed."

*Summary*

1. Our Lord in the Temple is the consecration of the Christian school.
2. The finding in the Temple was a double joy to Mary, in the Child, and in His work.
3. But there had been sorrow, which must have had a cause; that cause is the lesson it taught mankind.

## XXVII.—THE SUBJECTION OF JESUS

*"And He went down with them, and came to Nazareth, and was subject to them."—Luke ii. 51.*

1. He had finished this particular work which His Father had given Him to do. He had sanctified religious instruction; He had, in this simple event, provided for all time a proof that

## THE SUBJECTION OF JESUS

indeed He was more than man, that His discovery of Himself, as some modern critics would assert, was no gradual process, but that He knew Himself and His mission from the beginning; to go on from that moment teaching, to begin His public life at the age of twelve, would not have been in accordance with His fixed plan, of living the complete life of man, of bearing all man's burdens, of being "in all things like to man, sin alone excepted." Most men must live out their lives in hiddenness and seclusion; then our Lord must let men see that He would do the same. He has left us a complete account of these eighteen years—eighteen years, let us reckon it in our own lives, is a long time —but He has left it complete in only two short sentences.

2. "He went down to Nazareth, and was subject to them." In this, then, there was no change of plan. He was still "about His Father's business"; that is the one consistent thread that runs through His whole life; the one and only claim He makes at the end when He cries "Father, I have finished the work Thou gavest Me to do." But there is a change of another kind. "When I was a child," says St. Paul of himself, "I thought as a child; but when I became a man I put away the things of a child." And the same is true of Jesus. Hitherto He had been subject to His parents, but now for the first time is it said that He "was subject

to them." And rightly, for the subjection of a child to its parents scarcely deserves that name; it is rather affectionate dependence. But when the child has grown up and still obeys; when the boy, the youth, the full-grown man still keeps his parents in the first place, considering them, serving them, working for them, then we have free obedience. And this we have from this time forward in our Lord; at the age of twelve He "put away the things of a child," but He "was subject to them" none the less.

3. We look into human hearts, we look through history, we look at the first disaster of all, and we ask ourselves the cause of all the misery, in individual souls, in the whole world. Detailed and detached causes are many; but the one great disorder underlies them all; it is that of insubordination, disobedience. Adam disobeyed and fell; mankind disobeys and falls; the nations bring themselves to grief by encouraging disobedience; however sweet the fruits of liberty, however noble the ideal of freedom, still that heart is a corrupted heart, and a source of hopeless misery, to itself and to all who come under its influence, which acknowledges no master, which obeys no law. Obedience is the bond of union, the source of strength, the safeguard of peace, the power in action, the tree that bears fruit both material and spiritual. But it is a hard lesson for independent human nature to learn; no wonder, then, that the Savior of the

## THE GROWTH OF JESUS

world chose to teach it at such great expense.

*Summary*

1. Our Lord above all things wished to be "in all things like to man."
2. Hence, like man, He was subject; not only as a Child, but also of His own free choice.
3. At this cost He taught the lesson that most needs to be learned, obedience.

## XXVIII.—THE GROWTH OF JESUS

*"And Jesus increased in wisdom, and age, and grace with God and men."—Luke ii. 52.*

1. We cannot hope in a short meditation to fathom the meaning of this simple sentence. It has given rise to endless opinions among the Fathers of the Church, to endless discussions among theologians, and even the contemplative saints have given it various interpretations. But there are certain fundamental truths which all accept, and upon these it is possible to build enough material to supply a saint's meditations all his life. Our Lord was God and man. As God He did not and could not grow in any way; in this nature His knowledge, His wisdom, His grace were the same from all eternity; He was as God full and complete even when He lay helpless in the manger. But as man He could and did grow; as man He was limited, even as are all men; we watch the Child's body being fed and increasing in the natural way, the Boy's body "waxing strong," the body of the full-grown man, first resisting cruel treatment, and

finally being beaten by torture and dying like any other.

2. And as His body grew, so did such knowledge and such mental experience grow as depended primarily upon the body. With us men, placed and circumscribed as we are, all our knowledge depends in some way upon the body; as the philosophers say: "There is nothing in the intellect which is not first in the senses." Our eyes, our ears our sense of touch, etc., are the means by which we grow in understanding; we learn the facts of this life, we draw from them their essence, and with this essence we arrive at our conclusions. So was it with the Holy Child. As a Child He "lived and learned." St. Paul tells us that "He learned obedience from the things that He suffered"; and we may add that He learned many other things as well. He learned above all what human life was as we human beings learn it. And as He learned so He showed this growth in His life; as it were He kept His Divine understanding in check, while He lived as a true Man among men. And His Mother watched the growth, and marvelled at, and recorded it.

3. "Jesus increased in wisdom." Wisdom includes many things; it includes depth of insight, breadth of understanding, sagacity of judgment, prudence of counsel. We learn in the hope that learning will make us wise; we pass through experiences of many kinds, and every

experience, will, if we will let it, make us wiser. In this sense did our Lord increase. "Jesus increased in age." Age has different stages. The virtues of the Child are not those of the youth; those of the youth are not the virtues of the full-grown man. So did our Lord increase. As a Child He was a child, and acted as a child; as a Boy, He acted as a boy; among men He was a man, "all things to all men," "in all things like to man," so that throughout His career His fellow Nazarenes had noticed nothing strange, unnatural, not even as it seemed supernatural, about Him. "Jesus increased in grace with God and men." In grace with God because at each step in life He "did the work His Father gave Him to do"; in grace with men, if only for the simple reason that the perfect saint is the perfect man. "He hath done all things well," was the verdict of the crowd early in His public life.

### Summary

1. Our Lord could not "increase" in any way as God; but He did "increase" as Man.
2. He grew in body, He grew in mind, He showed that growth in His life.
3. He grew in wisdom, and age, and grace, as all men grow.

## XXIX.—OUR LADY OF NAZARETH

*"And His Mother kept all these words in her heart."*—Luke ii. 51.

1. Scholars consider themselves amply justi-

fied in concluding from the evidence that these two chapters of St. Luke have been drawn from Our Lady's own lips, and are even the very words of Our Lady herself; and the repeated statement that she "kept all these words in her heart," is taken as signifying that St. Luke took the narrative from her. She was a soul of not many words. Wherever we meet her, except on one occasion, she does little more than stand by and look on; when she does speak it is in the full and measured words of one who has an instinct to keep silence rather than to express herself at all.

2. On the other hand, the one occasion on which, as it were, she lets herself speak from her full heart, shows both the matter and the depth of her meditation. The Magnificat teems with Scripture references. No one could have uttered that wonderful prayer who had not (1) pondered long on the words of Holy Scripture, (2) seen their application to and fulfilment in the Messiah, (3) led her thoughts on from the consequences of His coming to the whole world. The same is seen in the Angel's words at the Annunciation; he is speaking to one who, he knows, thinks along this definite line. This, then, we may safely take it, is Our Lady's "method" of meditation; from Scripture to our Lord, from our Lord to men, with herself affected by the conclusion as the "Handmaid of the Lord." God promised, God redeemed, God spread

*OUR LADY OF NAZARETH*

the fruits of the redemption among men; and so long as this was done all was done. From this her "practical conclusion" was easily drawn; it was that she should dispose herself to be used by Him in whatever way He chose for this end, as His simple "Handmaid."

3. Hence when later we find her saying of herself that she "kept all these words, pondering them in her heart," we have little difficulty in following her mind. She took each scene in her Child's life as it opened out before her; she gathered up every word that was spoken concerning Him. In each event she saw the guiding and redeeming hand of God; in every word she heard the echo of the voice of God. Both alike she interpreted in the light of her Son, seeing in them greater significance because He was the central figure, knowing that because of Him everything had its meaning, its purpose, its power, its lesson. The question: "Why hast thou done so!" was not once only, but continually in her heart. And for answer, as we see unmistakably in the Magnificat, she looked beyond the ages, and reflected on the fruit all this would bear to all mankind; the good tidings of great joy that it would be to all the people, so that all generations would bless the Lord for blessing her; the thoughts that out of many hearts would be revealed, making her agony, whatever it might be, worth while; the numbers that would give up all, and would set about their Father's

business, just because her Son had said the word, and given the example, in giving up even her, His dearly loved Mother.

*Summary*

1. Our Lady is a soul of few words.
2. But a soul of much meditation; and the matter and manner of her meditations are not difficult to discover. "To restore all things in Christ," might be given as their common title.
3. Hence one may easily estimate what it was she kept in her heart.

## XXX.—ST. JOSEPH

*"And when there also they began to be famished, the people cried to Pharao for food. And he said to them: Go to Joseph; and do all that he shall say to you."—Gen. xli. 55.*

1. The Holy Family is the model of all family life; the reproduction of the life of the Holy Family among men is the surest guarantee of contentment and prosperity in this world and of happiness in the next; where nations are most happy there we find the closest resemblances to the Holy Family in the houses of their citizens; the fallacy of much modern legislation, of many modern tendencies, and of many more modern cravings, lies precisely in this ignoring and elimination of the spirit of the Holy Family from the home. And the head of the Holy Family is not the Child, nor the Mother,

## ST. JOSEPH

but St. Joseph. It is, then, no wonder that as the ages have advanced, as the struggle of Christianity has more and more converged round the defense of the family, the figure of St. Joseph should have emerged more and more from its natural place of retirement, and should have been set in the front of the battle-line, and that he should have become the patron of family life.

2. If we look into the secrets of this Holy Family, we cannot but be struck with the love which bound it together. "We shall know only in heaven what Joseph was to Mary and Mary to Joseph." The initial material for affection that was in both, the consecration to one another by the hand of God Himself, the sharing of the care of the Child Jesus, the companionship, faithful and unstinted, in many mutual sorrows and anxieties, "for better for worse, for richer for poorer, in sickness and in pain," the love returned to them both by the Child that stood between them, the trust He placed in them, the confidences He gave them, the kindness He received from them and returned in His own way, and on the other side the utter devotedness of the foster father, who had no thought for himself, but only for the charge entrusted to him, all these things compel us to the peace of that Holy Family, and to affection for Joseph its protector, who kept that house a house of joy, no matter what vicissitudes it had to undergo.

*THE PRINCE OF PEACE*

3. But of another phase of life is St. Joseph patron, and that is its end. After the finding in the Temple we hear of him no more; when the public life begins, at Cana of Galilee, and at other places where his presence would seem to have been essential, he does not appear; the conclusion is that some time during the eighteen years of the hidden life he passed away. His work of protection was done; Jesus was now able to look to Himself and to provide for His Mother; then God took Joseph away. He had lived a perfect life, he had done a perfect work, in the doing of that work his own soul, unnoticed by himself—so devoted was he to others— had been made a perfect thing; the most perfect, the Church permits us to believe, that the angels have ever carried to heaven. To him the end came; in the arms of Jesus and Mary he passed away, the most perfect of deaths, closing the most perfect of lives, a thing of sweetest agony, a thing of agonizing sweetness, as a truly happy death cannot but always be to those who know and have felt what is life and what is love.

*Summary*

1. The Holy Family is the model of family life, and St. Joseph is its head and patron.
2. The secrets of the Holy Family, founded in love, extol the soul of St. Joseph evermore.
3. St. Joseph, the patron of a happy life, is also the patron of a happy death.

# Daughters of St. Paul

IN MASSACHUSETTS
 50 St. Paul's Ave., Jamaica Plain, Boston, MA 02130; **617-522-8911; 617-522-0875**
 172 Tremont Street, Boston, MA 02111; **617-426-5464; 617-426-4230**
IN NEW YORK
 78 Fort Place, Staten Island, NY 10301; **212-447-5071**
 59 East 43rd Street, New York, NY 10017; **212-986-7580**
 625 East 187th Street, Bronx, NY 10458; **212-584-0440**
 525 Main Street, Buffalo, NY 14203; **716-847-6044**
IN NEW JERSEY
 Hudson Mall — Route 440 and Communipaw Ave., Jersey City, NJ 07304; **201-433-7740**
IN CONNECTICUT
 202 Fairfield Ave., Bridgeport, CT 06604; **203-335-9913**
IN OHIO
 2105 Ontario St. (at Prospect Ave.), Cleveland, OH 44115; **216-621-9427**
 25 E. Eighth Street, Cincinnati, OH 45202; **513-721-4838**
IN PENNSYLVANIA
 1719 Chestnut Street, Philadelphia, PA 19103; **215-568-2638**
IN VIRGINIA
 1025 King St., Alexandria, VA 22314  **703-683-1741**
IN FLORIDA
 2700 Biscayne Blvd., Miami, FL 33137; **305-573-1618**
IN LOUISIANA
 4403 Veterans Memorial Blvd., Metairie, LA 70002; **504-887-7631; 504-887-0113**
 1800 South Acadian Thruway, P.O. Box 2028, Baton Rouge, LA 70821 **504-343-4057; 504-343-3814**
IN MISSOURI
 1001 Pine Street (at North 10th), St. Louis, MO 63101; **314-621-0346; 314-231-1034**
IN ILLINOIS
 172 North Michigan Ave., Chicago, IL 60601; **312-346-4228 312-346-3240**
IN TEXAS
 114 Main Plaza, San Antonio, TX 78205; **512-224-8101**
IN CALIFORNIA
 1570 Fifth Avenue, San Diego, CA 92101; **714-232-1442**
 46 Geary Street, San Francisco, CA 94108; **415-781-5180**
IN HAWAII
 1143 Bishop Street, Honolulu, HI 96813; **808-521-2731**
IN ALASKA
 750 West 5th Avenue, Anchorage AK 99501; **907-272-8183**

IN CANADA
 3022 Dufferin Street, Toronto 395, Ontario, Canada
IN ENGLAND
 128, Notting Hill Gate, London W11 3QG, England
 133 Corporation Street, Birmingham B4 6PH, England
 5A-7 Royal Exchange Square, Glasgow G1 3AH, England
 82 Bold Street, Liverpool L1 4HR, England
IN AUSTRALIA
 58 Abbotsford Rd., Homebush, N.S.W., Sydney 2140, Australia